D1934861

Ursula Le Guin

A Very Long Way

Text and Study Aids

Edited and annotated
by Inta Wirth

Ernst Klett Schulbuchverlag
Stuttgart Düsseldorf Berlin Leipzig

Herausgegeben von Inta Wirth, Bietigheim-Bissingen.

About the Author

Ursula K. Le Guin is a well-known writer of science fiction and fantasy novels. *A Very Long Way*, originally titled *Very Far Away From Anywhere Else*, is an exception among her works in that it is not set on a distant planet in the future but in a contemporary American environment – an ordinary town somewhere on the West Coast – and that it features adolescent protagonists of our world. Nevertheless, certain themes that recur in her science fiction are treated in this short novel as well. Owen's utopia "Thorn" is an example.

Ursula K. Le Guin was born in Berkeley, California in 1929. Her father, A. L. Kroeber, was a professor of anthropology at the University of California at Berkeley and her mother was a writer. Both parents encouraged her to read and develop her imagination. Ursula first attended Radcliffe, a college for women associated with Harvard University, and then Columbia University, graduating with an M.A. in French. In 1953 a Fulbright grant gave her the opportunity to study in France. Here she met Charles Le Guin and married him. They have three children and now live in Portland, Oregon, where her husband is a professor of history at Oregon State University and where she teaches creative writing classes besides working on her own publications.

Gedruckt auf Neoprint, hergestellt von Stora Papyrus aus chlorfrei gebleichtem Zellstoff, säurefrei.

1. Auflage 1 5 4 3 2 1 | 1996 95 94 93 92

Alle Drucke dieser Auflage können im Unterricht nebeneinander benutzt werden. Die letzte Zahl bezeichnet das Jahr dieses Druckes.
Copyright © 1976 by Inter-Vivos Trust for the Le Guin Children; this edition published by arrangement with Virginia Kidd Literary Agent. Title of the original edition: Very Far Away from Anywhere Else.
Copyright © für diese Ausgabe: Ernst Klett Schulbuchverlag GmbH, Stuttgart 1992. Alle Rechte vorbehalten.

Redaktion: Dr. Hartmut K. Selke, Verlagsredakteur.

Satz: Setzerei Lihs, Ludwigsburg
Druck: Gutmann + Co., Heilbronn
ISBN 3-12-577310-5

Contents

How to Read This Book 4

A Very Long Way (Text and Annotations) 6

Additional Texts

1. American Education *(Douglas K. Stevenson)* 57
2. A Game Called Dating *(Margaret Mead)* 61
3. The Stage of Adolescing *(Erik H. Erikson)* 63
4. The Role of the Peer-group *(David Riesman)* 65
5. Women in the Musical World *(Eva Rieger)*. 66
6. The Image of Women in Advertising *(Lucy Komisar)* 67

How to Read this Book

Ursula Le Guin's novel *A Very Long Way* is not meant to be read, say, like a poem by Shakespeare. Rather, it is to be read quickly and extensively, and you should enjoy your quick progress in the book. The necessity to look up words in a dictionary – or even in the annotations at the bottom of the page – can be demotivating and prevent your reading pleasure. For this reason, we have decided to explain only those words that are absolutely necessary and that cannot be guessed with the help of one of the four techniques described below. The method described here follows that suggested by Peter Bruck in *The Wave* (Klettbuch 57728).

1. Word Family

Sometimes words unknown to you are made up of elements that you are familiar with. First try to identify the *root word*, e.g. "change" in "interchangeable" (p. 13, l. 23). The *prefix* "inter-" means "between" or "reciprocally" and the *suffix* "-able", that you are surely familiar with, means "capable of " or "which can be". An "interchangeable part" is therefore one which can be exchanged for another.

2. Similar German, French or Latin Words

Make the best use of the other languages (including your own!) that you already know. For example "nightingale" (p. 8, l. 30) is quite similar to German "Nachtigall".

3. Context

Examining the *context* in which a word appears, i.e. the words or sentences before and after it, is by far the most important technique. Take the word "licence" in "I had learned to drive, and got my licence in October" (p. 10, l. 1). Quite obviously, "licence" must be a document which says that you can drive a car and are allowed to do so. In this case the context provided by one sentence is enough to help you guess the meaning of the word. Now look at "exsanguination" in the sentence "Death by exsanguination" (p. 12, l. 19). Unless you can guess the meaning of the word from your knowledge of Latin or French, the context provided by the sentence alone is not guite enough and you have to look three paragraphs further up to guess the meaning of "exsanguination", i.e. "bleeding to death".

4. Sound

Sometimes the meaning of a word becomes clear when it is spoken aloud, as in this sentence: "He said it with real hatred, hissing" (p. 8, l. 27). But, as a look at the line will show, context is a help here, too.

So as to give you an easy start, the words whose meanings can be found with the help of the techniques described above have been marked with a number in the first 30 pages of the novel.

1 – words that can be guessed from the word family (e.g. fame)
2 – words that can be guessed from similar German, French or Latin words (e.g. fortune)
3 – words that can be guessed from the context (e.g. dull)
4 – words that can be guessed from the sound (e.g. hissing)

And now – have fun!

A Very Long Way

If you'd like a story about how I won my basketball colours and achieved fame[1], love, and fortune[2], don't read this. I don't know what I achieved in the six months I'm going to tell about. I achieved something, all right, but I think it may take me the rest of my life to find out what.

I never won any colours for anything. When I was a little kid I really liked football, the strategy[2] of it, but being short for my age I was always a bit slow even though I was good at evasive tactics. And then when we got into high school it all got so organized. Going out for teams and wearing uniforms and all that stuff. And people talk about it all the time. Sports are neat to do, but dull[3] to talk about. Anyhow, there won't be much about sports in this.

I am talking into a tape recorder and then typing it. I tried to just write it, but it came out all stuffy and clotted-up with words, so let's see how it goes this way. My name is Owen Thomas Griffiths. I was seventeen in November. I am still fairly short for my age – 5 feet 7 inches. I guess I will be short for my age when I'm forty-five, so what's the difference? It bothered me a lot when I was twelve or thirteen, but I was much shorter then compared to other kids, a genuine shrimp. At fifteen I grew six inches in eight months and felt really awful while I was doing it; my knees used to feel like the Bamboo Splinter Torture[2], but when it was over I was such a giant compared to what I had been that I never could really regret not going on any higher. I am average compact[2] build and have dirty grey eyes and a lot of hair. The hair is curly and whether I wear it short or long it sticks out all over my head. I fight it with a hairbrush every morning, and lose. I like my hair. It has a lot of willpower. However, this story is not about my hair, either.

I am always the youngest person in my class. And the youngest person in my family, being the only child. They let me start school a year early because I was such a bright little jerk. I have always been bright for my age. Who knows, at forty-five I may still be bright for my age. That

1 **to win your colours** in sports: to be chosen as a member of a team – 7 **football** i.e. American football – 8 **evasive tactics** [ɪ'veɪsɪv] moving in such a way as to avoid the opponent's attack – 11 **neat** *here:* fun, nice – 14 **stuffy and clotted up with words** unnatural and said with too many words – 19 **shrimp** *(coll.)* a small person (usual meaning: *Krabbe*) – 30 **jerk** [dʒɜ:k] *(sl.)* a stupid or disagreeable person

is partly what this thing I'm telling, this story, is about. About being a bright little jerk.

It's O.K., you know, while you're in primary school. Nobody really cares, least of all yourself. The teachers are mostly pretty nice to you, because you're easy to teach. Some of them love you for it, and give you interesting books for extra reading. Some of them resent[3] it, but they're too busy with the Behaviour Problem types to have time to really make you feel lousy for being ahead of the others in maths and reading. And there's always a few other kids, usually girls, who are as smart as you are, or smarter, and you and they write the class skits, and make lists for the teacher, and so on. And besides, for all the talk about how cruel little kids are, they haven't got a patch on older people for cruelty. Little kids are just dumb, the smart ones and the slow ones. They do dumb things. They say what they think. They haven't learned enough yet to say what they don't really think. That comes later, when kids begin to turn into people, and find out that they are alone.

I think what you mostly do when you find you really are alone is to panic. You rush to the opposite extreme and pack yourself into groups – clubs, teams, societies, types. You suddenly start dressing exactly like the others. It's a way of being invisible. The way you sew the patches[3] on the holes in your jeans becomes incredibly important. If you do it wrong you're not with it.[3] You have to be with it. That's a peculiar phrase, you know? With it. With what? With them. With the others. All together. Safety in numbers. I'm not me. I'm a basketball colour. I'm a popular kid. I'm my friends' friend. I'm a black leather growth[1] on a Honda. I'm a member. I'm a teenager. You can't see me, all you can see is us. We're safe.

And if We see You standing alone by yourself, if you're lucky we'll ignore you. If you're not lucky, we might throw rocks. Because we don't like people standing there with the wrong kind of patches on their jeans reminding us that we're each alone and none of us is safe.

I tried. I really did. I tried so hard it makes me sick to think about it. I did my jeans patches exactly like Bill Ebold who did everything right. I talked about baseball scores. I worked for the school paper for one term,

10 **class skit** short funny scene acted out in class – 12 **they haven't got a patch on older people for cruelty** *(coll.)* they aren't nearly as cruel as older people – 20 **invisible** [ɪn'vɪzəbl] who or which cannot be seen – **to sew (sewed, sewn)** [səʊ] to join pieces of cloth together with a needle and thread – 34 **score** number of goals, runs or points in a game

because that was the one group that I could figure out how to get into. But none of it worked. I don't know why. Sometimes I wonder if introverts have a peculiar smell, which only extroverts are aware of.

Some kids really don't have much Me at all. They truly are part of the group. But a lot of them just act – pretend – the way I tried to. Their heart isn't really in the groups, but still they get along, they get by. I wish I could. I honestly wish I could be a good hypocrite. It doesn't hurt anybody, and it sure makes life easier. But I never could fool anybody. They knew I wasn't interested in what interested them, and they despised me for it, and I despised them for despising me. But then I also despised the few kids who didn't try to go along. In fourth year there was this tall kid who never brushed his teeth and wore a white sports coat to school, who wanted to make friends with me. I should have been delighted; I mean, nobody had ever wanted to make friends with me before. But he kept saying things like what a drip[3] this person was and what a dolt[3] that one was, and although I agreed with him I didn't want to talk about it all the time, and so I despised him for being a snob. And then I despised myself for despising everybody else. Oh, it's a really neat situation to be in. You know what I mean, if you've been there.

Since I was trying hard not to be different, I didn't want to be top of the class; but that problem was always solved for me by gym. I wasn't any worse at gym than a lot of fellows, but I got low marks because I cut it all the time because I couldn't take Mr Thorpe. 'If you can take your mind off Keats and Shelley for a while, Griffiths, you might at least stand around and *watch* how basketball is played.' It was always Keats and Shelley – I heard him use exactly the same line to at least two other fellows. He said it with real hatred, hissing[4]: *Keatsssnssshelley, ssssss.* It was stupid applied to me, since maths and science is where I am good, but that hatred got me so curious I went back and read Keats's 'Ode to a Nightingale'[2]. They didn't give us any Shelley, but I looked up his collected works at the city library, and later on I bought it second-hand. So it was Mr Thorpe teaching basketball who put me on to 'Prometheus

7 **hypocrite** ['hɪpəkrɪt] a person who pretends to have feelings, beliefs or principles he or she doesn't have – 10 **to despise** [dɪ'spaɪz] to have a low opinion of s.o. – 14 **delighted** [dɪ'laɪtɪd] very happy – 21 **gym** [dʒɪm] gymnastics – 22 **to cut (classes)** *(sl.)* to miss classes without being excused – 24 **Keats** John Keats, English poet (1795–1821) – **Shelley** Percy Bysshe Shelley, English poet (1792–1821). Both are representatives of the romantic period. – 28 **to apply s.th. to s.o./s.th.** to use a word or phrase to refer to s.o./s.th.

Unbound'. I should be grateful. But it still didn't make third period with Mr Thorpe any easier.

But – this is important – I never talked back. I never said anything. I could have said, 'Look, Mr Thorpe, I don't want to take my mind off Keats and Shelley, or sines[2] and cosines[2], so you just go ahead and bounce[3] your little bouncyball, O.K.?' Some of the kids could do that. Back in primary school once I heard a little black girl tell off our maths teacher, 'You just get your hands off my paper, if you don't like it the way I done it you can just stuff it!' It was pure fight – the teacher hadn't done anything to deserve it, he was just trying to teach the kid some maths – but still, it was pure fight, it was courage, and I admired it. I still do. But I can't do it. I haven't got it. I don't get into fights.

I stand there and take it, till I can run. And then I run.

Sometimes I not only stand there and take it, I even smile at them and say I'm sorry.

When I feel that smile coming onto my face, I wish I could take my face off and stamp on it.

It was five days after my birthday. I was seventeen and five days. Tuesday, 25 November. Raining. I took the bus because it was raining so hard when I got out of school. There was only one seat left. I sat down and tried to get the back of my neck away from my collar, which had got wet while I waited at the bus stop and felt like the Icy Hand of Death. And I sat there and felt guilty. About taking the bus.

Guilty about taking the bus. About taking the *bus.* Listen, the really terrible thing about being young is the triviality[2].

The reason I felt guilty about taking the bus is this. It was five days since my birthday, right? For my birthday my father had given me a present. A really fantastic present. It was unbelievable. He must have planned it and saved for it for years, literally. He had it there waiting when I got home from school. It was parked in front of the house but I didn't even notice it. He kept hinting, but I didn't get the hints. Finally he had to take me out and show it to me. When he gave me the keys his face got all twisted up as if he felt like crying with pride and pleasure.

It was a car, of course. I won't say the brand name because I think there's enough advertising around already. It was a new car. Clock, radio, all the extras. It took him an hour to show me all the extras.

9 **stuff it** *(sl.)* go to hell – 29 **literally** ['lɪtərəlɪ] in fact, truly

I had learned to drive, and got my licence[3] in October. It seemed useful, if there was an emergency, and I could do some errands for my mother, and get off by myself that way. She had a car, my father had a car, now I had a car. Three people, three cars. Only the thing was, I didn't want a car.

What did the thing cost? I didn't ask, but it was at least three thousand dollars. My father is a Chartered Accountant and we don't have that kind of money for unnecessary things. For that kind of money I could have lived for a year or more at the Massachusetts Institute of Technology, if I got a tuition scholarship. That's what came into my head right away, before he'd even opened the shiny little door. He could have put the money into savings. Of course, I could sell the car, and not take too bad a loss on it if I did it soon. That came into my head too, and that was when he put the keys in my hand and said, 'She's all yours, son!' and his face twisted up that way.

And I smiled. I guess.

I don't know if I fooled him. If so, it was probably the first time I had ever succeeded in fooling anybody; but I think so, because he wanted so badly to be fooled, to believe that I was struck dumb with joy and gratitude. That sounds as if I was scornful of him. I don't mean it that way.

We took the car out for a ride right away, of course. I drove up into the Park, and he drove it back – he was itching to get his hands on the wheel – and all that was fine. The trouble came when he found out on Monday that I hadn't driven my new car to school. Why not?

I couldn't tell him why not. I only half understood it myself. If I drove the thing to school and parked it in the school car park, I'd given in. I owned it. It owned me. I was the owner of a new car with all the extras. People at school would say, 'Hey, how about that. Hey wow. How about Fastback Griffiths!' Some of them would sneer, but some of them

2 **errand** short trip made to get necessary things done (e.g. shopping) – 7 **chartered accountant** a person whose job it is to keep a record of the money a business receives or spends – 9 **Massachusetts Institute of Technology (M.I.T.)** famous university in Cambridge, Mass., specializing in science subjects – 10 **tuition** [tjuːɪʃn] fee charged for attending college – **scholarship** ['skɒləʃɪp] financial aid given to a good student by the government or some other institution – 19 **to be struck dumb** [dʌm] to be made speechless – 20 **gratitude** ['grætɪtjuːd] thankfulness – **to be scornful of s.o.** to look down on s.o. with contempt – 23 **he was itching to do s.th.** he couldn't wait to do s.th. – 27 **to give in** to admit that you are defeated – 30 **fastback** streamline form of a fast car – **to sneer** to show contempt by an expression on your face or a way of speaking

would honestly admire it, and maybe me for being lucky enough to own it. And that's what I couldn't take. I didn't know who I was, but I knew one thing: I wasn't the seat-fixture of an automobile. What I was was the type who walks to school (it's 2.7 miles by the shortest route) because walking is the kind of exercise I like, and I really like the streets of the city. The pavements, the buildings, the people you pass. Not the brake lights on the back of the car in front of yours.

Well, anyhow, that was where I drew the line[3]. I'd already tried very ingeniously to hide the line, by driving errands for Mother on Saturday, and volunteering to take both my parents for a drive in the country on Sunday in 'my new car'. But Monday evening he found the line. Didn't you take the car to school? Why not?

So there I was on Tuesday on the bus feeling guilty. I wasn't even walking, after all my explanations of how I liked to walk and doctors say the exercise of walking is the best of all for the human body. I was on the bus. For twenty-five cents. And three thousand dollars' worth of car was sitting on its white sidewall steel-belted radials in front of our house, right where I'd get off the bus.

I looked out of the window of the bus to make sure it really was raining hard enough to be an excuse for not walking. It was coming down so hard that the bus windows looked like pebble glass; but mere facts don't seem to help guilt much. I wondered how my father would say, 'Didn't you take the car to school? Why not?' tonight. The thought made me twitch, and while twitching I noticed that the person in the window seat was somebody from school. I said, 'Oh, hi,' and she said, 'Hi,' and I wished it was somebody I didn't know so I could ignore her.

The Fields had lived in a house two blocks up our street for a couple of years, and Natalie had been in some classes with me last year. She had long dark hair and was quiet and you never saw her around and she did something with music, and that was one hundred per cent of what I knew about Natalie Field. She was good-looking, but I find almost all girls good-looking, so I am no judge. People wouldn't call her beautiful, because she was stocky, and had a severe expression; but I think she was good-looking, only you didn't notice it, because she wasn't noticing

3 **fixture** ['fɪkstʃə] a piece of furniture or equipment that is firmly installed – 9 **ingenious** [ɪn'dʒiːnɪəs] extremely clever – 17 **radial** ['reɪdɪəl] a type of tyre – 21 **pebble glass** glass with an uneven surface (e.g. as used in bathroom windows) – 24 **to twitch** to make a short, nervous movement – 33 **stocky** physically short and broad – **severe** [sɪ'vɪə] serious, strict

you. However, this time I did notice it, because she was noticing me. She had to. My knapsack flap had got wet through and was dripping onto her knee. I moved it so it would soak[3] into my thigh instead and said, 'Sorry. It's only a severed artery[2], it'll stop soon.'

Now that is really strange, that I said that. Normally I would have said 'Sorry' in a mumble and moved the knapsack and left it at that. I think that I was so sick of myself, of being guilty about the car, and being angry, and being lonely, and wondering what good it was being seventeen when it was just as bad or a little worse than being sixteen, and all the rest of it, that I drove myself out of myself. Anything to escape! Even being funny with some girl I didn't know. Or maybe there was something about her that made me speak, that made it possible for me to speak. Maybe when you meet the people you are supposed to meet you know it, without knowing it. I don't know.

She gave a laugh, a real laugh, surprised and tickled. So I went on, 'It's either seven seconds or fifteen seconds, from the femoral artery, I can't remember which.'

'What is?'

'Death by exsanguination[3]. Gggggghhh.' I slumped[4] down in the bus seat and died quietly. Then I sat up and said, 'Yechh, my collar's wet, it's like an ice pack.'

'Your hair's all wet, it's dripping on your collar.'

'I'm a drip,' I said with real feeling.

'Say,' she said, 'are you in Mr Senotti's history class? Is he all right?'

'He's all right. Tough. Bad temper. Comes of being called Mr Snotty, maybe; you can't blame him.'

'I have to take social sciences next term and I need a really easy teacher.'

'Don't take Snotty then. Take Vrebek, all she does is show movies.'

'I had her. That's why I quit. Oh, I don't know. Bah!' She really said 'Bah!' – exactly as spelt – but savagely. 'I hate easy classes, and I haven't got time to work hard for good teachers,' she said. Talking to herself more than to me. But my ears were really standing up on end. In twelve years of school I had never heard any human being say they hated easy classes.

2 **knapsack** ['næp-] bag carried strapped over one's back – 4 **severed** ['sevəd] cut through – 16 **femoral artery** ['femərəl ɑ:tərɪ] the chief artery of the thigh – 23 **drip** a dull or stupid person (here a play on words) – 31 **savagely** ['sævɪdʒlɪ] wildly, with a lot of force

'How come you got no time?' I said. 'Femoral artery severed? Remember, don't panic, you may have all of fifteen seconds.'

She laughed again, and she looked at me. Just for a moment. But she looked, she saw. She wasn't looking at me to see what she looked like, she was looking at me to see what I looked like. That is unusual, in my experience.

I got the impression, even then, that people didn't often say funny things to this girl, that she wasn't used to clowning[1], but she liked it. The peculiar thing was that I wasn't much used to clowning, either. With people I didn't know well – which was the entire human species except for my parents and Mike Reinhard and Jason Thoer – I was either completely speechless, or said extremely serious things that instantly prevented any further conversation. But still, I am male, and it seems to me that at our age acting funny is almost an instinctive form of behaviour in men. The girls laugh *at* things, but they seem basically serious. Whereas the fellows horse[3] around and clown and make everything into a joke. My only real relationship with Mike and Jason, who were the nearest thing I had to friends, was a joking relationship. The point was never to be serious about anything. Except maybe sports scores. One of the main subjects to talk about was sex, but we kept unserious about sex either by telling dirty jokes, or by being gross[3] – using the special technical vocabulary of the sexual engineer, as if women were machines with interchangeable[1] parts. I was pretty good at the dirty jokes, but my engineering vocabulary was unconvincing.

I might as well say here that at fifteen I still didn't know what 'scoring with a girl' meant. I thought it meant you'd gone out and had a good time at a movie or a party or something. I knew the facts of life, all right, but I didn't connect that phrase with them. So that when Mike, who was way ahead of me physically, started telling us that he had finally scored with this girl, I said, 'Yeah, what did you do?' And he gave me this look and said, 'What do you think we did?' and I have never felt so stupid in my life. I am getting red talking about it into this tape recorder. Mike had to go and tell a lot of other fellows about me asking, 'What did you do?' It was good for lots of humour. However, they forgot about it eventually, and I kept a good string[3] of dirty jokes worked up, so that I could talk with Mike and Jason. It beat eating lunch alone, I guess.

1 **How come ...?** *(coll.)* Why ...? – 24 **unconvincing** not believable or plausible – 35 **eventually** [ɪˈventʃʊəlɪ] finally, in the end – 36 **It beat ...** *(sl.)* It was better than ...

But one more thing about humour and seriousness: it doesn't necessarily go on like that. Older women sometimes say the funniest things, and older men often get deadly serious. My father has no sense of humour left at all. He is a kind man, but nothing ever strikes him as funny. But I've heard my mother and her friend Beverley laughing, in the kitchen, till they were bumping[4] around like drunks and gasping[4]. And they were laughing about something dumb Beverley herself had done. Just listening to them whooping[4] in there made me laugh, for nothing, for pleasure.

Well, anyhow, it was really neat to have this girl laugh like that at my feeble jokes, so I went on. 'Sounds to me as if what you need is two aspirin tablets and a tourniquet. Bring the leg in to me tomorrow. We have a three-legged centaur that needs a transplant[2].' And so on. I mean feeble. But she laughed at me till I ran out; and then I said, 'But how come no time? You got a job?'

'I give some lessons.'

I couldn't remember what instrument she played. It would be uncool to ask. 'You like it?'

She shrugged and made a face. 'Oh, well, it's music,' she said. Like people say, 'Oh, well, it's a living.' But the implication[1] is different.

'That's what you want to be, a music teacher?'

'No,' she said, the way she'd said 'Bah'. 'No teacher. Just music.'

She was so fierce she sounded like Tarzan, but it wasn't directed at me, exactly. She had a nice voice, clear and soft, with that fierceness in it. I went into an ape act. 'No teacher. Urgh, urgh, kill teacher. Good teacher, yum yum. No teacher. Good tummy, fat, full of teacher.' Natalie said, 'Teacher lousy, all bones!' The man across the aisle was giving us Send to Siberian Prison Camp Look No. 12. That kind of look can create a bond between you. 'What are you going in for?' Natalie asked.

'Urgh, urgh, professional gorilla. Taking Advanced Grooming now, in Home Economics,' and I showed her how to groom my knapsack and

11 **feeble** weak – 12 **tourniquet** ['tʊənɪkeɪ] tight kind of bandage that stops bleeding – 13 **centaur** ['sentɔ:] a mythological creature that is half man and half horse – 17 **uncool** *(sl.)* not "with it" – 19 **to shrug** to pull up one's shoulders to show that one does not know s.th. – 23 **fierce** angry, forceful – 26 **tummy** *(coll.)* stomach – 27 **aisle** [aɪl] passage leading through the middle of a bus – 29 **bond** feeling of friendship that unites people – **to go in for s.th.** to be interested in s.th. – 31 **to groom** to clean an animal's fur

eat the fleas neatly. Then I said, 'I'm going to be a teacher.' That seemed even funnier for some reason than the ape act, and we both laughed.

'Honestly?'

'No, I don't know. Maybe. Something. Depends where I go to college, I guess.'

'Where do you want to go?'

'M.I.T.'

'Mental Institute of ... Texas ...'

'Massachusetts Institute of Technology. Or else Cal Tech. Science. Laboratories, acres of laboratories. White rats. Dedicated men in white coats laboriously[1] sneaking up sideways[1] on the secrets of the Universe. Frankenstein's monster. All that.'

'Yeah,' Natalie said. She didn't say it questioningly, or agreeing-without-understanding, or mocking, or meaning nothing. She said it firmly. That's it. Yeah. 'That's neat,' she said.

'It's also expensive.'

'Oh, well,' she said, 'you can always handle that.'

'How?'

'Scholarships – working – that's why I'm giving lessons. So I can get to Tanglewood this summer.'

'Tanglewood, New South Wales?'

She gave a laugh-snort and said, 'It's a music school thing.'

'Near the Mental Institute of Texas. Yes.'

'Right.'

It was my stop. I got up and said, 'So long,' and she said, 'So long,' and I got off in the rain. Only after I got off I thought I could have ridden on two more blocks with her, to her stop, and we could have sort of finished the conversation. It had ended so fast. I jumped up and down in the rain doing the ape act as the bus started up again, but she was on the other side of the bus; nobody saw me but the Director of Siberian Prison Camps, and he looked away quickly and winced.

1 **flea** a small jumping insect that feeds on the blood of animals or people – 8 **mental institute** psychiatric clinic – 10 **dedicated** believing in s.th. and giving a lot of time and effort to their work – 11 **to sneak up on s.th.** to move towards s.th. very quietly to surprise it before it can escape – 14 **to mock** to make fun of, to ridicule – 31 **to wince** to make a slight movement as if in physical or mental pain

The reason I have reported that conversation on the bus with Natalie Field so exactly is that it was an unimportant conversation that was extremely important to me. And that's important, that something unimportant can be so important.

I guess I tend to think that important events should be solemn, and very grand, with muted violins playing in the background. It's hard to realize that the really important things are just normal little happenings and decisions, and when they turn on the background music and the spotlights and the uniforms, nothing important is going to happen at all.

What stuck in my head after that conversation was just one word, the most commonplace[1], meaningless word. It wasn't the way she looked, or the way she looked at me, or my acting like a clown and making her laugh, or it was all that, but all sort of compressed[1] into one word, 'Yeah,' the way she said it. Firmly, certainly. Yeah, that's what you're going to do. It was like a rock. Whenever I looked into my head there was this rock.

And I needed a rock. Something to hold on to, to stand on. Something solid[2]. Because everything was going soft, turning into mush[4], into marsh, into fog. Fog closing in on all sides. I didn't know where I was at all.

It was really getting bad. It had been coming for a while, for a long while I guess, but it was the car that really brought it on.

You see, in giving me that car my father was saying: 'This is what I want you to be. A normal car-loving American teenager.' And by giving it to me he had made it impossible for me to say what I wanted to say, which was that I had finally realized that that's what I wasn't, and was never going to be, and I needed help finding out what I was instead. But to say that, now, I had to say, 'Take your present back, I don't want it!' And I couldn't. He'd put his heart into that gift. It was the best he could possibly give me. And I was supposed to say, 'Take yourself back, Dad, I don't want you?'

I think my mother understood all that, but in a way that wasn't any use to me. My mother was and is a good wife. Being a good wife and mother is the important thing in her life. And she is a good wife and mother. She never lets my father down. She nags him about some

5 **solemn** ['sɒləm] very serious – 6 **muted** playing very softly – 36 **to nag** to complain in an irritating way

things, of course, but she never sneers at him or cuts him down, the way I've heard women do to their husbands; in all the big things she backs him up – what he does is right. And she keeps the house clean and cooks really well and makes extra stuff like biscuits and muesli and when you want a clean shirt there is one and when Muscular Dystrophy or some other charity organization wants a co-ordinator or a door-to-door collector she does it. And if you think all that, running even a small family and house so that things are decent and peaceful, is a small job, maybe you ought to try it for a year or two. She works hard and uses her head at it. But the trouble is, she's afraid of doing anything else, of being anything else. Not afraid for herself, I think, but afraid that if she did anything except look after us, she'd be letting us down – letting the side down, not being a good wife and mother. She feels she's got to be always there. She can't even take off the time it takes to read a novel. I think she doesn't read novels because if she got really interested in one, absorbed[3], then she'd be somewhere else, by herself: she wouldn't be with us. And that's wrong, to her. So all she ever reads are some magazines about food and interior[2] decorating and one about extremely expensive holiday travel to places she doesn't want to go to. My father watches a lot of TV but she never pays much attention to it; she may be sitting there with him in the living room, but she's sewing or doing crewelwork or figuring out household stuff or working on Muscular Dystrophy lists. Ready to get up and do what needs doing.

She didn't spoil[3] me, more than an only kid always gets spoiled by being the centre of attention. She used to try to keep me from reading so much, but she sort of gave up when I was twelve or thirteen. As far back as I can remember, I had to keep my room straight and do garden jobs. I do the lawn and carry out rubbish and so on. Male jobs only, of course. I never learned how to work the washing machine till the time she had to have an operation and couldn't climb stairs for two weeks. I don't think my father knows how to work it yet. That's woman's work. It's funny, really, because he's nuts about machines. All our appliances have to have about twelve different cycles and all possible attachments. If he

5 **muscular dystrophy** [ˌmʌskjʊlə ˈdɪstrəfɪ] a serious disease in which the muscles become gradually weaker (capital letters: name of a charity) – 6 **charity** [ˈtʃærɪtɪ] organization which raises money to help people who are very poor, ill or handicapped – 8 **decent** [ˈdiːsnt] respectable – 22 **crewelwork** [ˈkruːəl-] a kind of embroidery – 32 **to be nuts about s.th.** *(coll.)* to be very enthusiastic about s.th. – **appliance** [əˈplaɪəns] household machine

ever bought the plain ordinary model of anything he'd feel he wasn't treating her right. But if they're household work machines, she runs them. And when they break down, she calls the repairman. My father doesn't like to hear about things breaking down.

That's why I couldn't say anything about the car. Because it had really broken me down. It just was the end, the last stop. I had to get off. But there wasn't anything outside the bus but rain and fog and me jumping up and down doing an ape act and nobody looking or hearing.

I came in from the bus stop that day. My mother was in the kitchen blending something in the blender. She yelled something over the scream of the machine but I couldn't hear what. I went up to my room and dropped my knapsack and took off my coat with the wet collar and stood there. The rain was whacking[4] on the roof. I said, 'I am an intellectual. I am an intellectual. I am an intellectual. And the rest of you can go to hell!'

I heard my voice and it sounded unbelievably feeble. Big deal! So I was an intellectual, and what else is new? That's when the fog closed in completely. And that's when I found the rock. It was actually like that, as if my hand closed around a solid, round rock. The girl on the bus saying, 'Yeah,' in that solid, round voice. Yeah: good. So go ahead and be what you are.

So when I had rubbed some of the rain out of my hair with a towel, I sat down at my desk and started to reread Ornstein's *The Psychology of Consciousness.* Because something like that, thinking about how we actually think, how our heads work, is what I would like to do.

But it didn't last. I dropped the rock. At dinner my father got going about how you break in a new car. You should drive it at moderate[2] speeds every day, and going to and from school would be perfect for it. 'If you want me to take it to work for a week or so of course I'll be glad to,' he said. 'It's not good for a new car just to sit there.'

'O.K.,' I said, 'you do that.'

That blew it. His face got tight. 'If you didn't want the car, you might have told me.'

'You never asked me if I wanted a car.'

His face got tighter, like a clenched[3] fist. He said, 'It's been driven very little. I suppose the dealer might take it back. Not for the full cost, of course. They couldn't resell it as new.'

10 **to blend** to mix – 16 **Big deal!** *(sl.)* So what! – 24 **consciousness** ['kɒnʃəsnəs] the mind – 27 **to break in** *(usu. a young horse, here: a new car)* to make it accustomed to use – 32 **That blew it!** *(sl.)* That ruined it. – 35 **fist** tightly closed hand

'Oh rubbish, what a notion,' my mother said. 'How is Owen to get back and forth from State every day next year without a car of his own? It would take him an hour each way on the bus. For goodness sake, Jim, don't expect him to start living in the car right off! If you want to drive it to the office, do. But it'll get plenty of use next year!'

That was fine. My mother is a highly intelligent person. She had just given my father his first practical reason for giving me a car – his excuse, his justification[3]. State University is right on the other edge of our city, about ten miles from where we live. I would certainly need a car to get to classes there next year. The only trouble was that State was not where I wanted to go to college.

But if I brought that up, if I said, 'What if I go away to college?' I'd have blown it again. We'd have had two quarrels going instead of one. Because it was my mother who was dead set on my going to State. And I do mean dead set. She'd gone there, she met Dad there, she quit before she'd finished the course to get married. She knew State. It was safe. The places I wanted to go weren't safe. They were far away, and she didn't understand what went on at them; they were full of communists and radicals and intellectuals.

I had applied to M.I.T., Cal Tech., and Princeton, as well as State. My father had filled out the scholarship applications and paid the application fees. The forms were incredible, all in quadruplicate[2], but being a Chartered Accountant, he rather enjoyed filling them out clearly and honestly, and he didn't mind the fees because I think he took some pride[1] in my shooting for the moon. I expect he mentioned to his friends at the office that his son was applying to Princeton. That was something to be proud of, especially if I didn't actually go there. But he said nothing about it to my mother, as far as I know, and she said nothing about it to either of us. If we wanted to throw away ninety dollars on fees, all right. But her son was going to State.

And she had a practical reason. A very sound one. They could afford to send me there.

1 **notion** idea – 2 **State** *here:* the State University – 14 **to be dead set on s.th.** *(sl.)* to be determined about s.th. – 20 **Cal Tech** California Institute of Technology at Pasadena, a small but prestigious school – **Princeton** famous and prestigious university in New Jersey – 22 **incredible** [-'---] unbelievable – 25 **to shoot for the moon** to aim for the highest goal; to try the impossible – 31 **a sound reason** a good reason

I didn't say anything. I couldn't. My jaws locked[3]. I couldn't swallow the piece of pot roast I'd been working on, either. It just lay there in my mouth, a fibrous sort of lump. I couldn't chew it. I worked it over to one side, and drank some milk around it, and after a long time I managed to chew it and swallow it. After a longer time dinner was over. I went up to do homework.

It was no good. Why should I study? What for? I could get to State without studying. I could probably get right through State without studying. I could probably go on and become an accountant or a tax auditor or a maths teacher and be respectable and successful and get married and have a family and buy a house and get old and die without ever studying, without ever thinking at all. Why not? A lot of other people did. You think you're so special, Griffiths.

I couldn't stand the sight of any of the books in my room, I hated them. I went downstairs and said, 'Going out for a drive,' around the ghost of that piece of beef that still seemed to be in my mouth, and I went out and got into the new car. I had left the keys in it, Sunday. Even Dad hadn't noticed. It could have been stolen any time during the last two days. If only it had been. I started it up and drove very slowly down the street. Breaking it in.

At the end of the second block I passed the Fields' house.

O.K., now I know I was sick – really sick, a little past the breaking point – that night, because of what I did. I did what any normal car-loving American teenager would do if he'd met a girl he liked. I stopped and backed and parked in front of the Fields' and went up to the front door and knocked and said to Mrs Field, 'Is Natalie here?'

'She's practising.'

'Can I see her for a minute?'

'I'll ask her.'

Mrs Field was a good-looking woman, older than my parents. She had the same severe expression Natalie had, but she was handsomer. Maybe Natalie would be that handsome at fifty. Kind of worn and polished[3] like a piece of granite in a creek. Mrs Field wasn't friendly or unfriendly, welcoming or off-putting[3]. She was calm. She just stated the facts. She stood aside – it was still raining – and let me into the hall; didn't ask me in any farther; went upstairs. As she went, I heard Natalie practising.

3 **a fibrous lump** ['faɪbrəs] a tough and dry mass – 9 **tax auditor** a person whose job it is to examine business accounts in order to find out whether a firm is paying enough taxes

It must be a violin, I thought. A tremendous[3] noise, even though the Fields' house was bigger than ours and older, with thicker walls. A big, sweet, hard, rushing noise, rushing down the scales like a creek over rocks, bright and fierce – and then it stopped. I'd stopped it.

I heard Mrs Field upstairs say, 'It's the Griffiths boy.' She knew us mainly because Mother had hooked[3] her last spring for a charity appeal[2], and she'd been at our house for the planning meeting.

Natalie came downstairs. She was frowning and her hair was all messed up. 'Oh hi, Owen,' she said from a distance roughly equivalent to the orbit of Neptune.

'I'm sorry I stopped you practising,' I said.

'That's all right. What's on your mind?'

I had been going to ask her if she'd like to go for a drive in my new car, but I couldn't. I said, 'I don't know.'

And the ghost of the piece of pot roast came back and filled my entire mouth.

She looked at me, and after this long, horrible silence she said, 'Is something wrong?'

I nodded.

'Are you sick?'

I shook my head. Shaking it seemed to clear it a bit. I said, 'I'm upset. It's something to do with my parents. And stuff. It's not terminal. But I. But I wanted to talk. But I. But I can't.

She was kind of floored[1]. She said, 'Would you like a glass of milk?'

'I've just eaten dinner.'

'Camomile[2] tea,' she said.

'Peter Rabbit,' I said.

'Come on in.'

'I don't want to interrupt you. Listen. Can I sit and listen to you practise? Would it bother you a lot?'

She hesitated[3], and then she said, 'No. You want to? It's dull.'

We went to the kitchen, and she poured me a cup of extremely weird tea, and then we went upstairs to this room. What a room! All the walls

3 **scales** a sequence of musical notes played in an upward or downward order – **creek** a very small river, brook – 8 **to frown** [aʊ] to move your eyebrows together as a result of anger or concentration – 9 **roughly** *here:* about, approximately – 10 **orbit** the path taken by a planet around the sun – 22 **terminal** about to cause death – 27 **Peter Rabbit** character in a series of children's books by Beatrix Potter (1866–1943) – 32 **weird** [wɪəd] strange, queer

in the Fields' house were dark, and it all looked kind of bare, kind of calm and severe like Mrs Field, but this room was the barest. It had in it one Oriental rug worn down to the warp[3] or whatever you call it so you could hardly see what colours it had been, and one grand piano, three music stands, and a chair. There were some stacks of music under the windows. I sat down on the rug. 'You can sit in the chair,' she said, 'I stand up to practise.'

'I'm fine here.'

'O.K.,' she said. 'This is some Bach. I have to cut an audition tape next week.' And she picked up her fiddle off the piano and injected[3] it under her jaw in that peculiar way violinists do – only I figured out from the size that this one was a viola not a violin – and rubbed her bow with rosin and stared at the music on the music stand and started playing.

It wasn't your standard concert performance. For one thing the room was so high and bare that it made the noise loud, hard, so that it sort of rang in your bones (she said afterwards it was a perfect room for practising because she could hear all her mistakes). And she made faces and muttered a lot. And she would play the same bit over and over and over. That crashing[4] run she'd been doing when I came in, she must have done it ten or fifteen times, sometimes going on from it, but coming back to it again, starting over. And every time it was slightly different. Until finally it came out the same twice in a row. She'd got it right. Then she went on. Then when she played the whole movement over, that part sounded the same the third time in a row. Right. Yeah.

It had never occurred to me before that music and thinking are so much alike. In fact you could say music is another way of thinking, or maybe thinking is another kind of music.

They talk about the patience scientists have to have, and how scientific work is 99% drudgery[3] and repetition and neatness and making perfectly sure. And it is. I had a very good bio teacher last year, Miss Capswell, and she and I did some lab[1] work after school in spring term. We were working with bacteria[2]. It was exactly the same thing Natalie was doing with the viola. Everything had to be right. You didn't know for sure what was going to happen when you finally did get it all right: you had to get it right to find out. Miss Capswell and I were trying to

9 **to cut an audition tape** to make a recording so others can judge the quality of your performance – 13 **rosin** ['rɒzɪn] brown resin derived from the sap of pine trees and used to increase sliding friction on the bows of certain stringed instruments

confirm[2] an experiment reported in *Science* magazine last year. Natalie was trying to confirm what Bach had reported to some church congregation in Germany 250 years ago. If she did it absolutely right, it might turn out to be true. To be the truth.

That was maybe the most important thing that happened to me that day – understanding that.

After about forty minutes of practising, she started on a sticky fast part and fought with it for a while and got mad at it and went YAARKHH! on the strings and quit. She sat down on the rug too, and we talked. I told her what I had been thinking about music and thinking, and she liked it; but she asked didn't a scientist have to keep feeling out of his thinking, whereas in music they were the same thing. That didn't seem exactly right to me but we couldn't figure out just what did happen in science. I told her about working with Miss Capswell and how neat it had been, because this was the first person I had ever met who just took it for granted you were interested in ideas. Working with her in the lab had been just about the first time in my life I didn't feel like an outsider, or self-conscious, or fake; and it was really because of that that I'd realized that no matter how I tried I was never going to be an extrovert, or popular, or one of the group, so I might as well quit trying. But Miss Capswell got transferred[2] to another school over the summer and when I came back in the autumn, school was even worse than it had been before, in a way, because I wasn't even tormenting myself with trying to be part of it any more, so there wasn't anything left at all. I didn't tell Natalie all that, that evening, of course. But we did talk a bit about school, about conformity[2] and why it is hard to be different. She said it seemed like the only choices offered were to want to be what other people were, or to be what other people wanted you to be. Either to conform, or to obey. And that got me on to the car, and college, and my parents. She listened, and she understood perfectly about the car, but not so well about college. She said, 'Well, O.K., but you wouldn't actually give up going to the place where you belong, and go to a school you don't want? I mean, why?'

2 **congregation** [ˌ--'--] people attending a church service – 16 **to take s.th. for granted** to accept s.th. as natural – 18 **self-conscious** uncertain of yourself, nervous – **fake** not real, deceptive – 23 **to torment s.o.** to be cruel to s.o.

'Because they expect me to.'

'But they expected wrong, didn't they?'

'I don't know. There's money, too.'

'There's loans and scholarships.'

'There's a lot of competition.'

'You're telling me,' she said, fairly sarcastically. 'So you have to compete. All you can do is try, isn't it?'

She was hard to answer. But not the way my parents were. They were hard to answer because you could never get to the real point with them, and she was hard to answer because she'd got there first. But at least she didn't leave me fighting a piece of phantom pot roast. Her mother brought us up some other kind of weird tea, and we talked some more, just sort of nothing, friendly talk, and at ten-thirty I left, figuring she might want to practise some more, because she'd said she tried to practise three hours a day. I drove around a few blocks and got home and went to bed. I was really tired. Like I'd walked a hundred miles. But the fog was gone. I went to bed and straight to sleep.

All that was on 25 November, like I said. Between then and New Year's Eve I got to know Natalie Field a good deal better. We got along well. Whenever we got together we started talking, and we talked like crazy for as long as we had. We didn't often have very long, because she was really busy. She gave lessons after school five days a week, and on Saturdays she worked from nine to two at a music school, teaching something called Orff Method to little kids, and at nights she practised, and Sundays she played in a chamber group, and practised, and went to church. Mr Field was a very religious man. No, I withdraw[3] that. Mr Field was a very churchgoing man. I don't know if he was a religious man or not. Natalie was a religious person, and she probably got it from him, but she didn't like church at all. She went, though. She had thought a lot about it and decided it was more important to her father than it was to her, so she'd give in on that point, as long as she lived at home. She thought things like that out. Sometimes going to church made her resentful, but she didn't get all bogged down and tied up in her resentment, the way I did over the car. She just swore about the dumb

4 **loan** a sum of money you can borrow – 33 **resentful** [-'--] full of bitterness – **to get bogged down** *(fig.)* to sink into depression (bog = swamp) – 34 **to swear (swore, sworn) about s.o./s.th.** to call s.o./s.th. bad names

minister and went on with what she had to do next. She had her priorities[2] straight.

She was eighteen, a year and a half older than me. That can make a big difference at our age, especially since girls are supposed to mature faster psychologically than boys, but it didn't matter to us. We just got along well. She was the first person I'd ever met I could really talk to, and talk with. The more we talked the more there was to talk about. We both had last period free, and we could hang around and talk then till she had to go to her lessons; and sometimes in the evening I went over, and then there was the Christmas holidays.

I think it wasn't till the holidays that I found out she wasn't studying to be a professional violinist. She played the viola and violin and piano, but what she wanted to be was a composer. She worked on the instruments so she could earn money teaching, and get into music schools, and later on teach or play in an orchestra for a living, but that was all just means to an end. It took me quite a while to find that out, because she was shy of talking about it. I'm not sure she'd ever told anybody about it except maybe her mother. She was so self-confident and realistic about her playing, I didn't realize at first that that covered up a whole area where she wasn't self-confident, and was ambitious and idealistic and ignorant and unsure, so that it was hard for her to talk about. But it was the real centre of her whole life.

'There aren't any women composers,' she said once. It was the Christmas holidays and we'd been able to see each other several times. We were walking in the Park that day. It's the best thing in our city, a huge park, a forest, with long hiking trails. We were walking the fat off Mrs Field's dog, a poopakeep[3] named Orville. It was raining.

I know that what results from crossing a toy poodle and a pekinese is a registered[3] breed called a Peke-A-Poo; but that dog was a poopakeep.

'No women composers? There's got to be some,' I said. She said there were, but they didn't amount to very much, or if they did you couldn't find out because if they wrote operas they didn't get staged[1], and if they wrote symphonies they didn't get performed. 'But if they were good, *really* good,' she said, 'they would get played, I think. There just haven't been any absolutely first-class ones.'

4 **to mature** [mə'tjʊə] to become fully developed – 8 **period** *here:* a lesson at school – 13 **composer** [kəm'pəʊzə] a person who writes music – 18 **self-confident** sure of your own abilities and worth – 29 **breed** type of animal (the poodle is a breed of dog) – 31 **they didn't amount to much** they weren't very good

'Why not?' It seemed peculiar when you thought about it. Popular music has a lot of women composers now, and most kinds of singing have always been half women; anyhow music doesn't seem male, it seems human.

'I don't know why not. Maybe I'll find out why not,' she said rather grimly[2]. 'But I *think* it's prejudice and stuff. Like the self-whatsit-thingo you told me.'

'Self-fulfilling prophecy?'

'Yeah. Everybody says you can't, and so you believe it. It was that way in literature, till enough women stopped listening and just wrote enough great novels that the men really looked like idiots if they went on saying women couldn't write novels. The trouble is, women have to be absolutely first class to get where third-class men get. It's weird. I guess it's the same thing as your Levellers[3].'

Talking with her, I had worked out this theory, see, about what it was that made me feel so much an outsider. Why it is that people make heroes out of people who are good at sports or politics, but have this scorn and resentment against people who are good at thinking. Unless the ideas they think turn directly into money or power, in which case they're heroes again. Anti-intellectualism seemed to be part of it but not all of it; it was this sort of pulling things all down to the level where everybody is the same, like ants, that I called 'Levelling', although these days it gets called by some fancy names like anti-elitism[2], and some really out of place names like democracy, names you shouldn't even say unless you're willing to think about them.

'Male Chauvinist[2] Levellers?' I said.

'Yeah, right on,' she said. Orville came back down the trail, running like a fourteen-inch-high pregnant cow, and got mud all over my jeans, and then got mud all over her jeans.

'What kind of music do you want to write?' I asked her.

She tried to tell me, but I can't tell you because frankly I understood less than half of it. I mean if you don't know pretty clearly what a tonal row is, you are not going to understand somebody explaining what's wrong with the theories about tonal rows. And I didn't want to interrupt her and make her explain, because it wasn't easy for her to talk about it at all, but she wanted to, very badly. She talked about order and

1 **peculiar** [pɪ'kjuːlɪə] strange, unusual – 6 **and stuff** *(coll.)* and things like that – 23 **fancy** special, elaborate – 28 **pregnant** ['pregnənt] expecting a baby – 36 **very badly** very much

humanity in music, and machine music, and random music, and I sort of understood that, but I didn't know enough about modern music to be sure I understood. But some of it I could make sense of, because it was very close basically to some things I'd been reading by some modern psychologists about identifying with machinery – people thinking of the world, and themselves, as machines. Schizophrenics now often do that literally. They have to be plugged into a power source in order to function, and they receive instructions from a Great Computer. Reading about them I had thought about some of the rock groups with their electronic instruments and mikes and consoles[2] and the stage full of wires, and the auditorium[2] full of people who plug in emotionally with them, all depending on one wire from the power plant. Who says schizophrenics are crazy?

It was something along that line Natalie was after – getting music away from its dependence on machinery, but by machinery she also meant the big symphony orchestra and the big opera production. But she didn't mean going back to 'simplicity', the folk singer with a dulcimer and a fake Kentucky accent. She said complexity[2] was essential[3] to high art, but the complexity ought to be in the music, not in the means of production. I said that sounded like Einstein doing it all with a pencil and some paper and his head, instead of a fifty-million-dollar accelerator; accelerators were very neat, but basically Einstein was even neater, and a lot cheaper. She really liked that. We turned back, and the sun came out and made all the wet forest look like crystal, and we went to her place, and she played me one of her compositions on the piano.

She explained that it wasn't for piano but for a string trio, and she sang the violin part in places. It didn't really seem very complex, or anyhow not difficult; there was a beautiful short tune in it that kept coming back, or pieces of it would come back, when things got rough. She was very tense, nervous, playing it; she was high. At the end she slammed the cover over the keys and said, 'The end's all wrong.' And then she had to go across town to give a lesson.

Natalie Field is very hard to describe. I guess anybody is. But typing up what I said about her into the tape recorder, I'm afraid it makes her

1 **random** without plan or pattern – 7 **to (be) plug(ged) in(to)** to (be) attach(ed) to a source of electricity – 12 **power plant** a factory that produces electricity – 14 **something along that line** s.th. like that – 17 **dulcimer** ['dʌlsɪmə] a folk instrument related to the guitar and plucked with the fingers – 22 **accelerator** [ək'seləreɪtə] *here:* a machine used in nuclear physics, e.g. a betatron

sound pompous. I guess when we talked we were both pompous, part of the time. Because we were talking about things that were very important to us, for the first time – saying stuff we'd never had anybody to say to. So it all sort of poured out unfiltered. And she was definitely a strong-minded person, self-reliant and very decisive. But then, because she'd worked so hard – and she really had, ever since she was six when she had taught herself the piano so that her parents had been sort of forced to start getting her lessons – because she'd worked so long and hard at one thing, music, she was pretty young and green about some other things. For instance she hardly ever went to movies. I took her to a Woody Allen, the one where he throws the cello out of the window, and I thought she was going to be sick she laughed so much. And the way she laughed at me when I clowned: she wanted to laugh, she needed to. All I had to do was go into the ape act, and she was helpless. Her father was this grim fundamentalist type, her mother was always calm and serene, her older sisters had both married and moved away, she worked and taught and practised and composed and dreamed music. There wasn't anything funny, anything ridiculous in her life, till I showed up. What I realize now is that she needed me just as badly as I needed her.

But I fouled it up. Because I got my priorities wrong.

Before that, though, there was the day at the beach. The good one.

It was the day before New Year's Eve. It had stopped raining, and got cold and clear and still. Heart of winter. When I woke up early the sun was shining the way it does way up high in the mountains, flooding down light out of a dark blue sky. I knew Natalie had the whole day free, because some of her pupils weren't taking lessons during the holiday. So I rang her up, and we decided to go over to the coast, in the new car.

It was O.K. with Mrs Field. She seemed to think I was O.K., as far as I could tell. Mr Field, who I gathered was extremely Biblical about young men who cast their eyes upon his daughters, was working – he was a building contractor – and didn't get home till around six. We'd be back before then, and what he didn't know wouldn't damage him irrepar-

1 **pompous** self-important, vain – 5 **self-reliant** independent – 11 **Woody Allen** (born 1935) U.S. actor and film director – 15 **fundamentalist** *(U.S.)* holding conservative religious beliefs based on a literal interpretation of the Bible – 16 **serene** [sɪ'ri:n] peaceful – 21 **to foul s.th. up** *(coll.)* to spoil s.th. – 33 **building contractor** a businessman in the construction industry

ably[1]. It was fine with my parents. All they knew was I was driving over to the coast with a friend. Mother was delighted that I had a friend, any friend, and Dad was delighted that I was doing something, anything, with the car. So everybody was happy, and we left at nine with a picnic lunch that Natalie had fixed.

It's about ninety miles over to the coast and ten miles south to Jade Beach, where I wanted to go. It's a cove between big headlands, not too windy, and not crowded even in summer. In winter it was completely deserted. Where there was some snow on the road in the Coast Range, I drove pretty slowly, so we got there about noon. The sky was completely clear and very bright; the Pacific was dark blue with high white breakers coming in fast. It was cold, but down on the beach the only wind was the wind that came in with the breakers[2]. The spray hit you like fine rocksalt. After a while you could take off your coat, if you kept moving. We did. We horsed around in the shallow breakers for a long time, and kept getting a little bit farther out. The water was like ice, but after the first moments of agony it felt good, in a numbing sort of way. I got wet from the neck down, Natalie got wet from the waist down. We came back up to a dry hollow by a big driftwood[1] log, and built a fire to get dry and eat lunch by. We ate a lot of lunch. I mean an unbelievable amount. When Natalie packed a lunch, she didn't cut corners. I don't know how many sandwiches there were to start with, but there were none to end with, and I ate three bananas, an orange and two apples. I might not have eaten so many bananas except that they became the cause of much youthful mirth and innocent merriment[1]. Honestly, I don't know why a basically sane person like Natalie was such a fall guy for the ape act. But true appreciation is the spur of genius, and the ape act definitely reached its highest moments that afternoon, with the assistance of the bananas.

Then we did some cliff climbing and some rock throwing, and built a sand castle. Then we came back and built up the fire, because it was getting colder, and watched the tide get closer to our sand castle, and

7 **cove** [kəʊv] a small bay – **headland** a narrow piece of land that sticks out into the sea – 9 **deserted** [-'--] without any people – 15 **shallow** ['ʃæləʊ] not deep – 17 **agony** ['ægənɪ] great pain or suffering – **numbing** ['nʌmɪŋ] making numb, i.e. unable to feel anything – 21 **to cut corners** to cut expenses, to try to save on money or effort – 25 **mirth** [mɜ:θ] *(lit.)* amusement, laughter – 26 **sane** not crazy – **fall guy** *(sl.)* a person who falls for s.th., i.e. is easily impressed – 27 **spur** a horse is kicked with a spur to make it go faster; *here fig.:* encouragement

talked. We didn't talk about problems, or parents, or automobiles, or ambitions. We talked about life. We decided that it was no good asking what is the meaning of life because life isn't an answer, life is the question, and you, yourself, are the answer. And the sea was there, forty feet away and coming closer, and the sky over the sea, and the sun going down the sky. And it was cold, and it was the high point of my life.

I'd had high points before. Once at night walking in the Park in the rain in autumn. Once out in the desert, under the stars, when I turned into the earth turning on its axis. Sometimes thinking, just thinking things through. But always alone. By myself. This time I was not alone. I was on the high mountain with a friend. There is nothing, there is *nothing* that beats that. If it never happens again in my life, still I can say, I was there once.

While we were talking we were sifting through the sand around where we sat for bits of jade[2] and agate[2]. Natalie found a black rock, flat, perfectly oval, and sand-polished. I found a lens-shaped agate, white and yellow; you could see the sun through it. She gave me the black rock, and I gave her the agate.

While we were driving home, she fell asleep. That was neat. That was like coming back down the high mountain quietly in the sunset. I drove well and carefully, quietly.

It was way past seven when we got home. We'd let time go on the beach. She slipped out of the car, still looking sleepy and windburned, and said, 'It was beautiful, Owen,' and went into her house smiling.

The Fields went out of town after that, and I didn't see Natalie till the day school started again. I waited for the bus with her. While we were hanging around there, I said I hoped her getting home late hadn't made any trouble with her father. She said, 'Oh, well.' And we talked about Ornstein's book; she was interested in his explanations about the silent half of the brain, where the music is.

But if I wanted to blame anybody but myself for what went wrong, I guess I would blame Natalie's father.

When she said 'Oh, well,' of course it meant that he had made some kind of stink, and she didn't want to talk about it, she preferred to ignore it or forget it. But what had he made a stink about, anyhow? She goes to the beach and eats lunch and finds an agate and comes home. This is wicked? This is sin? What did Mr Field have on his mind, anyhow?

It was perfectly obvious what he had on his mind.

That it wasn't what we had on our minds made no difference to him. You know these young people. All they're after is kicks.

So, O.K., I wasn't corrupted by Mr Field's obsessions. I wouldn't even have thought about them, if I hadn't been corrupted already. That's a funny word, isn't it, corrupted? My dictionary says it means 'To turn from a sound into an unsound condition ...' That's all I mean by it. I just got to thinking unsoundly.

The thing is, the way a lot of people talk, and the way a lot of movies and books and advertising and all the various sexual engineers, whether they're scientists or salesmen, tell you the way it is, is all the same. Man Plus Woman Equals Sex. Nothing else. No unknowns in the equation. Who needs unknowns?

Especially when you haven't had any sex yet at all and so *it* is the unknown, and everybody seems to be telling you that it's the only thing that matters, nothing else counts, and if you don't have sex all the time, you're either impotent or frigid and you'll probably get cancer within the year, too.

So I began thinking, what am I doing. I mean, I see this girl all the time and spend a whole day at the beach with her and somebody says, Hey man, so what happened? and I say: She gave me a black rock and I gave her an agate. Hey, yeah? Wow!

See, I began thinking what the others would think, not what I, myself, thought.

It's hard to explain, because there was more to it than that. Of course there was. Being with a girl, a woman, and Natalie was a woman, was exciting. That sounds dumb and you can make jokes about it if you want, but it's the right word. Physically, and mentally, and spiritually exciting.

But what I thought, because of what everybody, even Freud, says, was that it must be Love. They all say that sex is the real thing, and Love is what you call it when you are slightly more civilized than a gorilla. Sex isn't something you do when you're in love, love is what you call it when you want sex. Just ask the toothpaste commercials and the

3 **kicks** *(coll.)* pleasure, excitement – 4 **obsession** [əbˈseʃn] s.th. that you cannot stop thinking about – 7 **sound** *here:* healthy, undamaged – 17 **cancer** [ˈkænsə] a serious disease caused by a rapid increase of cells, producing abnormal growths *(Krebs)*

cigarette ads and the porno movies and the art movies and the pop songs, or Mr Field. Man, there is one important thing. Just one.

And so the next time we met, it was entirely different. I had decided that I was in love with Natalie. I hadn't fallen in love with her, please notice that I didn't say that; I had *decided* that I was in love with her.

According to some of the people who write about the brain and the mind, and who are interested in the front-back differences rather than the left-right differences, this would be an example of the frontal lobes trying to run the whole show, and fouling up the poor old hind-brain. This is a foul-up intellectuals are liable to. At least, stupid mixed-up intellectuals like me.

It was all right at first, because I was actually very cowardly. I spent the time when I wasn't with Natalie working on being in love with her. But when I was actually with her, I forgot about all that, and we talked like crazy, just like before.

One thing we talked about was our plans, a fairly natural subject for high school seniors in the last term. Hers were quite definite. She was going to Tanglewood this summer, mainly to meet people in the East, other musicians, professionals who might help her, and the other kids, the competition as she put it – she craved to meet the competition, to measure herself against them. Then she'd come back home in the autumn, and for one year she'd work full time at the music school and giving lessons to save money, and practising and composing, and taking a class at State in advanced theory and harmony; she said there was one man there who could teach her some things she needed to know; she'd already worked with him a bit, in summer school last year. Then she'd go to the Eastman School of Music in New York, with her savings and whatever scholarship they'd give her, and study with a couple of composers there 'for as long as it's worthwhile,' she said. This was the same kind of reason why I wanted to go to M.I.T.; there was a man there doing a kind of physiological psychology that was exactly what I was most interested in. We had some really strange conversations, with her explaining what these composers were trying to do and me trying to explain what consciousness was; but it was surprising how often the

8 **frontal lobes** the front sections of the brain – 9 **to run the whole show** *(coll.)* to be in charge – 10 **to be liable to (do s.th.)** ['laɪəbl] to tend to (do s.th.) – 18 **Tanglewood** an estate in Massachusetts where annual summer music festivals are held – 20 **to crave to do s.th.** to want very much to do s.th.

two completely different things came together and turned out to be related. The neat thing about ideas is the way they keep doing that.

In April the Civic Orchestra was giving a concert at one of the big churches, and three of Natalie's songs were to be on the programme. It was no big deal, she said; it was because she knew the conductor, and when he needed an experienced player to hold his amateur violinists together she did it for him; but still, it was a first public performance of her compositions. Composing, she said, is about the worst art of all, because it's about nine-tenths string-pulling. You have to know people, or you never get played. She was realistic about that, and said she wasn't going in for the 'Charles Ives game'. Ives heard hardly any of his music played in his lifetime, he just sat and wrote it and stuck it into a box and worked as an insurance broker or something. She disapproved of that. She said getting it played was part of the job. But she wasn't very consistent, because her two idols were Schubert, who never heard most of his big works, and Emily Brontë, who never really forgave her sister Charlotte for publishing her poems, or even in fact for reading them. The three songs that were to be performed in April were settings of Emily Brontë poems.

Wuthering Heights was Natalie's favourite book, and she knew a lot about the Brontë family, these four genius children living in a vicarage in a village on a moor in the middle of Nowhere, England, a hundred and fifty years ago. Talk about being isolated! I read a biography of them she gave me, and I realized that maybe I thought I had been lonely, but my life had been an orgy of sociability, compared to those four. But they did have each other. The kind of frightening thing was that it was the boy, the only son, who couldn't take it, and cracked up – went on drugs and alcohol, got hooked, and died of it. Because they'd all expected the most of him, because he was the boy. The girls, of whom nothing was expected since they were only girls, went on and wrote *Jane Eyre* and *Wuthering Heights.* It makes you think. Maybe I was not so unlucky in having parents who expected less of me than I wanted to give, after all. Maybe also it is not an unmixed blessing to be born male.

11 **Charles Ives** (1874–1959) American composer – 13 **insurance broker** a person whose job it is to sell insurance policies – 15 **consistent** [-'--] true to your own principles – 16 **Emily Brontë** ['brɒntɪ] (1818–1848) **Charlotte Brontë** (1816–1855) two of the three Brontë sisters (they are best known for their novels but also wrote poetry) – 21 **vicarage** ['vɪkərɪdʒ] house where a vicar, i.e. a priest in the Church of England, lives – 28 **to get hooked** [hʊkt] to become dependent on drugs – 33 **blessing** s.th. good that you are thankful for – **mixed blessing** s.th. that, although generally good, has one or more disadvantages

What the Brontë kids did for years was write stories and poems about these countries they made up. Maps, and wars, and adventures, and all. Charlotte and Branwell had 'Angria', and Emily and Anne had 'Gondal'. Emily burned all her Gondal stories when she realized she was going to die of TB, but by then Charlotte had made her save the poems. They all learned how to write, they practised it, by writing these long, involved romances about non-existent countries, for years. It came as a shock to me, because between twelve and sixteen I had done sort of the same thing, though I had no sister to show it to.

I had this country called Thorn. I drew maps of it and stuff, but mostly I didn't write stories about it. Instead I described the flora and fauna, and the landscape and the cities, and figured out the economy and the way they lived, their government and history. It started out as a kingdom when I was twelve, but by the time I was fifteen or sixteen it had become a kind of free socialistic set-up, and so I had to work out all the history of how they got from autocracy to socialism, and also their relationships to other nations. They weren't at all friendly with Russia, China, or the United States. In fact they traded only with Switzerland, Sweden and the Republic of San Marino. Thorn was a very small country, on an island in the South Atlantic, only about sixty miles across, and a very long way from anywhere else. The wind blew all the time in Thorn. The coasts were high and rocky. Sailing ships had very seldom been able to land there; the Greeks or Phoenicians had found it once, which gave rise to the myths of Atlantis, but it wasn't rediscovered until 1810. They had still, intentionally, not built a harbour for big ships, or any kind of landing field for planes. Fortunately it was small enough and poor enough that the Great Powers hadn't yet bothered to bring it into a sphere of influence and make it into a missile base. They let it alone. I had spent a lot of time on Thorn, for four years. But for over a year I hadn't been back; it all seemed long ago, kid stuff. Still, when I happened to think about it, I could see the steep cliffs over the sea, and the wind blowing over the long sheep pastures, and the city of Barren on the south coast, my favourite city, built of granite and cedar-wood, looking out over the windy cliffs to the Antarctic Ocean and the South Pole.

6 **involved** *here:* complicated – 24 **Atlantis** a legendary island, first mentioned by Plato, believed to have existed in the Atlantic Ocean – 28 **missile** ['mɪsaɪl] a rocket with a warhead – 32 **pasture** ['pɑːstʃə] land with grass growing on it for animals to graze on

I dug out some of the History of Thorn and showed it to Natalie. She really liked it. She said, 'I could write their music. You never talk about their music.'

'It's all wind instruments,' I said, clowning.

'O.K.', she said. 'A wind quintet. No clarinets. They're too sticky for Thorn. Flute, oboe, bassoon ... horn? English horn? Trombone? Yes, they'd have trombones ...' She wasn't clowning. She did write a wind quintet for Thorn.

Her definiteness about her plans infected me. It was catching. I began seriously thinking about what I would do if I could. Whether I wanted to go the medical route, or go into biology and work up to the place where bio and psychology interact, or go straight into psychology. They all fascinated me. They were all related, but you couldn't study them all at once, you'd just flounder. The question was where to start. Where to build up a solid foundation of knowledge on which you could balance ideas. It wasn't exactly a modest ambition. But what I had learned from Natalie was that you could have a very immodest ambition if you went after it methodically.

All that, talking about our plans, and music and science, and Thorn and Gondal, was great. Sometimes she played me a new bit of the Thorn Quintet. She had an old cornet trumpet she'd picked up for a dollar at a rummage sale, and she'd blow at it with her cheeks getting red and her eyes popping out, trying to let me hear a theme. I'd played cornet for one year in the primary school band, my entire musical career, but I could do about as well as she could. We fooled around with it and made it do all sorts of peeps and squeals and farts, and I performed 'The Isle of Capri', sort of. Once I drove her out to her Saturday job at the music school and hung around while she put the kids through their Orff Method, which was also great. Everybody had a xylophone or a bell or wood blocks, and when they all got going, fourteen six-year-olds with all that equipment, it was move over, Mick Jagger. She insisted that they learned music theory from it. I suggested that what they mostly got was a good time, and considerable hearing impairment if they kept it up long. Then we drove back and had a milk shake and French fries on the way and got to her house and her father was there.

6 **bassoon** [bə'su:n] musical instrument *(Fagott)* – **trombone** [trɒm'bəʊn] musical instrument *(Posaune)* – 14 **to flounder** to get lost, confused – 16 **modest** *here:* opposite of extreme – 31 **to insist** to say firmly – 33 **considerable hearing impairment** rather serious damage to their hearing ability

He didn't exactly say hello to me. He said hello to her, and looked at me.

And I got red and the smile came onto my face, the smile I wish I could stamp on. And I remembered that I was in love with Natalie. And so I couldn't say anything to him, or to her. I got sticky and uptight, and pretty soon I went home, where it was a lot easier and more comfortable to be in love.

I only saw Natalie three or four times in the next couple of weeks. And when I did it was much less enjoyable. I kept wondering things like whether she had ever had another man friend, and what she planned to do about men in among her other plans, and what she thought about me in that particular way, and not daring to ask her any of it. The closest I got was once when we were walking the fat off Orville again in the Park. I said, 'Do you think people can combine love with a career?' It came out and sort of hung there like a corpse. It sounded exactly like a question out of some magazine for Home-Makers. Natalie said, 'Well, of *course* they can,' and gave me an extremely peculiar look. Then Orville met a Great Dane on the path and tried to kill and eat it. When that was over we had got past the stupid question. But I kept on being sort of solemn and moody. As we were coming home Natalie said in a sort of wistful voice, 'How come you never do the ape act any more?'

That burned me. That really burned me. When I got home I was in a foul mood. What I want to do is take this girl suddenly in my arms and kiss her and say 'I love you!' and what she wants is for me to jump around with a banana peel looking for fleas in it.

I worked myself up good and proper. I resented her for being so friendly and matter of fact, and I deliberately thought about the way her hair looked when she'd just washed it and it was all sleek and soft, and the texture of her skin, which was white and very fine. And pretty soon I had managed to develop her into the real thing, the mysterious female, the cruel beauty, the untouchable desirable goddess, you name it. So that instead of being my first and best and only real friend, she was something that I wanted and hated. Hated because I wanted it, wanted because I hated it.

In February we drove over to the coast again.

5 **uptight** [-'-] tense, uncomfortable – 15 **corpse** [kɔ:ps] dead body – 18 **Great Dane** very large kind of dog – 20 **moody** depressed, gloomy – 21 **wistful** with longing – 26 **to work o.s. up** to become excited or angry – **to resent** to feel bitter about – 27 **deliberately** [-'----] on purpose – 28 **sleek** smooth and shiny

There's always a week around Washington's Birthday that is fantastic. It stops raining. The sun gets warm. The leaf buds start showing on the trees, and some first flowers come out. It's the first week of spring, and in some ways the best, because it's the first, and because it's so short.

You can count on that week, and I'd planned ahead. I got her to get a substitute at the music school and postpone her lessons, so that we could drive over to Jade Beach on Saturday. If her father made any static about it, I didn't care. She had to handle him. We were adults, and she had to learn to do without his approval for everything. I was all ready to tell her exactly that, if she mentioned her father; but she didn't. She didn't seem very enthusiastic about this trip, but I guess she knew I wanted it, so she did what I wanted, like a friend.

When we got to the beach about eleven in the morning, it was low tide, and there were some people clamming. We'd worn shorts under our jeans this time, and we played in the surf again, but it was different. There was a low fog over the sand, not thick and cold, just a kind of dimming as if the air was made of mother-of-pearl, and the waves were quiet and broke slowly, curving over themselves in long blue-green lines, dreamy and regular and hypnotic. We didn't stay together, but drifted apart, wading in the breakers. When I looked, Natalie was way up the beach, walking slowly in the foam, kicking up spray. She walked a little hunched with her hands in her pockets, and looked very small and frail there between the misty beach and the misty sea.

The clammers left when the tide began to come back in. After about an hour Natalie came wandering back. Her hair was all tangled in strings and she kept sniffing. The sea air made her nose run, and we hadn't brought any tissues. She looked serene and distant, the way her mother always looked. She'd picked up some rocks, but most of them were the kind that are beautiful when wet, but nothing much when they dry. 'Let's eat,' she said. 'I'm starving.'

I'd built a fire with driftwood in the same place as last time, in the hollow sheltered by the big log. She sat down right by the fire. I sat down next to her. I put my arm on her shoulders. Then my heart started

7 **substitute** ['sʌbstɪtju:t] a person who takes your place or function – **to postpone s.th.** [pəs'pəʊn] to arrange for s.th. to take place at a later time than was originally planned – 10 **approval** [ə'pru:vəl] agreement – 15 **clamming** looking for clams, a kind of shellfish – 23 **hunched** slightly bent – 24 **frail** thin and weak – 28 **tissue** thin soft paper that you can use as a handkerchief – 33 **sheltered** protected

hammering in this terrifying way, and I felt really crazy and dizzy, and I took hold of her really hard and kissed her. We kissed, and I couldn't get my breath. I hadn't meant to grab her like that; I had meant to kiss her and tell her 'I love you', and talk about it, about love, and that was all. I hadn't thought any farther. I didn't know what would happen to me, that it would be like when you're in deep water and a big breaker hits you and pulls you over and down and you can't swim and you can't breathe and there is nothing you can do, nothing.

She knew when the breaker hit me. And I guess it scared her too, but she wasn't caught in it. Because she pulled free after a bit and drew back, away from me. But she kept hold of my hand, because she saw that I was drowning.

'Owen,' she said, 'hey, Owen sweetheart, Owen, don't.'

Because I was sobbing. I don't know whether it was crying, or because I couldn't breathe.

I came out of it gradually. I was still too shaken up to be embarrassed or ashamed yet, and I reached for her other hand, so we were kneeling in the sand face to face, and I said, 'Natalie, why can't – we're not kids – don't you –'

She said, 'No, I don't. I don't, Owen. I love you. It isn't right.'

She didn't mean morally right. She meant right the way the music or the thought comes right, comes clear, is true. Maybe that's the same thing as moral rightness. I don't know.

It was she who said 'I love you'. Not me. I never did say it to her.

I said what I'd said before, stammering – I couldn't stop – and pulling her towards me. All of a sudden her eyes got very bright, and she scowled, and pulled away and stood right up. 'No!' she said. 'I *won't* get into this bind with you! I thought we could manage it but if we can't, we can't, and that's it. That's all. If what we have isn't enough, then forget it. Because it's all we do have. And you know it! And it's a lot! But if it's not enough, then let it be. Forget it!' And she turned and walked off, down the beach to the sea, in tears.

I sat there for a long time. The fire went out. I went and walked up the beach by the foam line, till I saw her sitting on a rock over the tide pools at the foot of the northern cliffs.

25 **to stammer** to speak nervously, to stutter – 27 **to scowl** [skaʊl] to make an angry face – 28 **bind** *(coll.)* a difficult situation

Her nose was all red and her legs were covered with goose pimples and looked very white and thin against the barnacle-rough rock.

'There's a crab,' she said, 'under the big anemone.'

We looked into the tide pool a while. I said, 'You must be starving, I am.' And we walked back along the foam line, and built up the fire, and pulled on our jeans, and ate some lunch. Not very much, this time. We didn't talk. Neither of us knew what to say any more. There were ten thousand things going on in my head, but I couldn't say any of them.

We started home right after lunch.

About at the summit of the Coast Range, I found the one thing I thought needed saying, and said it. I said, 'You know, it's different for a man.'

'Is it?' she said. 'Maybe. I don't know. You have to decide.'

Then my anger came out and I said, 'Decide what? You've already decided.'

She glanced at me. She had that remote look. She didn't say anything.

The anger took over entirely, and I said, 'I guess that's always the woman's privilege, isn't it?' in this sneering, bitter voice.

'People make the real choices together,' she said. Her voice was much lower and smaller than usual. She started blinking, and looked away, as if she was watching the scenery.

I went on driving, watching the road. We drove seventy miles without saying anything. At her house she said, 'Good-bye, Owen,' in the same small voice, and got out, and went into the house.

I remember that. But nothing after that. Nothing until the following Tuesday.

It's called specific amnesia, and is quite common following accidents, severe injuries, childbirth, etc. So I can't tell you what I did. My guess is that, being extremely upset, and since it was only about four-thirty, I didn't want to go home, but just went on driving around, probably, so that I could be alone and think.

There's a steep hill between two suburban towns west of the city. I don't know why I was out there. I guess I was just taking whatever road

2 **barnacle-rough** rough because of shells sticking to it – 10 **summit** peak, highest point of a mountain – 16 **remote** [-'-] far away – 20 **to blink** to move your eyelids quickly (here, to prevent crying) – 27 **amnesia** [æm'ni:zɪə] partial or total loss of memory

turned up, but anyhow, apparently what I did was take a turn too fast on that hill.

A car behind me saw the car go off the edge and turn over, and they got help. Ambulance and all that, because I was out cold. Concussion, also dislocated a shoulder and had a whole lot of really weird bruises that came out green. I was lucky, as they say, since the car was a write-off.

By the time I came to, they had moved me into a hospital in the city, and after another day I could go home.

I don't remember anything about either hospital, except my mother sitting there and telling me that Jason had called twice, and that Natalie Field had come over. 'What a nice girl,' my mother said. It all seemed perfectly natural but quite uninteresting to me. The fog had really and truly closed in. I was so alone in it I didn't know there was anything or anybody else out there. Nothing mattered. It was the concussion, of course. But not only that.

The whole thing was very hard on my father. First, of course, when some strange voice calls up and says, 'We have your son here in the hospital with severe concussion and possibly brain damage,' that's a really great thing to have happen in the middle of the Saturday afternoon TV ball game. Then all the relief and thankfulness, Owen's going to be O.K. Then paying for having the wreck towed. And finding out the car is a total loss. And his wife says, 'Who cares about the car so long as Owen is all right!' and bursts into tears. And he *does* care about the car, but how can he admit it to himself after that? And how can he admit that he's terribly humiliated by the fact that his son can't even drive around a corner without falling off? He has to be grateful to the son for not getting killed. And he is. Only there are moments when he'd like to kill the son himself. So he comes in and tells him not to worry, the car was fully insured, no problem. Not to worry. Only getting insurance for a while, after this, is going to be terribly expensive, so maybe the best thing is not to try to replace the car right away. And the son lies there and says, 'Yeah sure that's fine.'

I had to stick around home for a couple of weeks because our doctor

4 **concussion** [kən'kʌʃn] the result of a hard blow on your head – 5 **bruise** [bru:z] – 6 **the car was a write-off** so badly damaged that it was not worth repairing – 22 **to have the wreck towed** [təʊd] to have the broken car removed by a special truck – 26 **to be humiliated** [hju:'mɪlɪeɪtəd] to be made to feel ashamed

said so long as there was some vision impairment it would be wiser. It was very dull because I couldn't even read, because of seeing double, but I didn't care. I didn't want to read.

Natalie came by once, on the Friday after the accident I think. Mother came upstairs, and I said I didn't want to see anybody. Natalie didn't come back. Jason and Mike came by on the weekend and sat around and told some jokes. They were disappointed because I couldn't tell them anything about the accident.

When I went back to school, it was no trouble to avoid Natalie. It had never really been easy to meet her, since she had to run such a tight schedule. All I had to do was go in late for lunch, and not be at the bus stop at 2.30, and I never saw her at all.

I should be able to explain to you why I did that, why I didn't want to see her, but I can't. Parts of it are obvious, I guess. I was ashamed and embarrassed and so on. I was also resentful and frustrated and so on. But those are all reasons and feelings, and I wasn't reasoning or feeling anything much at all. Things just didn't seem to matter very much. The main thing seemed to be to avoid pain. There wasn't any use trying to be in touch. I was alone. I'd always been alone. For a while with her I'd been able to pretend that I wasn't, but I was, and finally I'd proved it even to her, forced her to turn her back on me like all the others. And it didn't really matter. If I was alone, O.K., it was better to accept it, not pretend. I was a kind of person that just does not fit into this kind of society. To expect anybody to like me was stupid. What should they like me for? My big brain? My big, smart brain with the concussion? Nobody likes brains. Brains are very ugly things. Some people like them fried in butter, but hardly any Americans do.

The only place for me, actually, was on Thorn. Thorn didn't have much government in the usual sense, but they had some institutions people could join if they liked; one of them was called the Scholary. It was built part way up one of the highest mountains, out in the country. It had a huge library, and laboratories and basic science equipment and lots of rooms and studies. People could go there and take classes or teach classes, however it worked out best, and work on research alone or in teams, as they preferred. At night they all met, if they felt like it, in a big hall with several fireplaces, and talked about genetics and his-

10 **to run a tight schedule** ['ʃedju:l; A.E.: 'sk-] to have many appointments and things to do so you have little time left

tory and sleep research and polymers and the age of the Universe. If you didn't like the conversation at one fireplace you could go to another one. The nights are always cold in Thorn. There's no fog there up on the mountainside, but the wind always blows.

But Thorn was way behind me now. I'd never go back there. No way home. I was finally able to be realistic about myself. There was school to finish, and then next year at State, and the next year and the next and so on. I could do it. I was actually much stronger than I'd thought. Too strong. Man of steel. Pulled practically undamaged from a totally wrecked car. I could see no particular reason for going on and finishing school and going to State and getting a job and living fifty more years, but that seemed to be the programme. A man of steel does what he is programmed to do.

I'm not describing this well at all. What I keep leaving out, what I don't know how to say, what I don't even want to think about, is that it was horrible. The whole time, for weeks, every morning when I woke up, every night in bed, I wanted to cry, because I couldn't stand it. Only I could stand it, and I couldn't cry. There wasn't anything to cry about.

And there wasn't anything to do. I'd tried, twice. Once with Natalie. Once with the car. And neither try had worked. There was no way to change things. I wouldn't get caught again. If I couldn't make a friend, O.K., I'd get along without. If I couldn't absent-mindedly drive off a cliff and kill myself, O.K., I'd stay alive. One attempt had been just as stupid as the other.

I knew my mother was worried about me, but it didn't bother me much. What she wanted for me was to be (1) alive, (2) normal. I was alive, and I was doing pretty much everything she wanted me to do. If it didn't produce normality, it ought to at least produce a pretty good fifty-year imitation of it. She also wanted me to be (3) happy, but that rabbit I could not produce out of the hat for her. I didn't do any crazy things, or sulk, or quarrel, or go on drugs, or refuse to eat her biscuits and pies, or join the American Communist Party, or anything. I just stayed in my own room a lot and kept to myself, and I'd always pretty much done that. So she figured I couldn't be too unhappy; it was just a mood. I know she knew it had something to do with Natalie Field. As I said, my

1 **polymer** ['pɒlɪmə] type of chemical compound used in plastic materials – 31 **to sulk** to be silently angry or bad-tempered

mother is a highly intelligent person. But all that could be labelled after all as puppy love, growing pains, perfectly normal.

My father, who didn't really know what he wanted for me, was more worried about me than she was, though I don't know if he knew it. I knew it from the way he talked to me. Sort of formal and uncertain. He didn't know what to say to me any more. And I didn't know what to say to him. And neither of us could do anything about it. But what did it really matter anyhow?

One thing I did was take a lot of showers. You can be really alone in the shower with the water running loud and a lot of steam and fog. I also went to a lot of movies with Mike and Jason. Sometimes I borrowed Dad's car for going to the movies. We had both figured it was important that I drive again as soon as possible, so that I wouldn't get uptight. It wasn't easy – for him or me – the first couple of times, but it worked out fine (maybe this is one purpose of selective amnesia), and it was a sort of ray of hope for him. Maybe Owen wasn't a total loss. After all, a lot of teenage boys wreck cars. It's almost a virile kind of thing to have done.

One thing I couldn't do, though, was homework. It was just too pointless. I'd always been able to get by when I was bored with a course by just sort of throwing words around and dazzling the teachers, but now I was bored even with the maths course I had, and you can't get by in maths by throwing words around. I just stopped doing the assignments, and I cut the tests. Advanced maths courses are small, and the teacher noticed right away and tried to say something about it to me, but I just said, 'Yeah,' and mumbled. There's nothing a teacher can do, really. In my other courses they were so used to me being good that they didn't notice I wasn't being good any more; so long as I showed up in class they assumed I was the same as always. And I didn't cut much. I would have, because school drove me crazy, not so much the classes as the halls full of people all talking to each other and the way they watch you walk past and so on; but what else was there to do? If I stayed at home, my mother was there, and I couldn't walk around the city all day.

So March went by and most of April went by. All fog. Fog and movies.

1 **to label s.th.** to put a label on s.th., i.e. to attach a name to it – 2 **puppy** a young dog – **puppy love** romantic love that an adolescent feels for s.o. and which is not likely to last long – 17 **virile** ['vɪraɪl] manly, fitting for a man – 20 **to dazzle** *here:* to impress – 22 **assignment** [ə'saɪnmənt] *here:* homework, etc. – 28 **to assume** [ə'sju:m] to believe

I was walking home from school one afternoon by one of my variant routes, and passed the First Congregational Church. A sign outside it announced that on Friday night there would be the spring performance of the Civic Orchestra, Leila Bone, soprano, works by Robert Schumann, Felix Mendelssohn, Antonio Vivaldi, and Natalie Field.

It's a beautiful name: Field. I see the curve of a field on a summer-coloured hill, under the sky. Or the long furrows on a winter field, dark brown, throwing shadows in the long sunlight.

It hurt a lot. It hurt incredibly much, and not a clean hurt either, because half of it was envy, the lowest kind of envy. But no matter how low I got, and it was unbelievable to me how low it was, still there were a couple of things I couldn't do. One of them was, I couldn't not go to hear the first public performance of compositions by Natalie Field.

So as I walked on past the church, I already knew I had to go. But the idea of going, and going alone, of course, was part of the hurt. It seemed like the end of something. It was the last thing I had to do that meant anything, and it was just left over from the time before, when things used to mean something. After it, there wouldn't be anything left to do. Ever.

I got home and the mail had come. There was a letter for me from the admissions office of M.I.T. My mother had left it out on the chest in the hall, but she didn't say anything or ask about it. I took it up to my room and read it. It said I had been admitted and they would give me a full tuition scholarship. I should at least have felt a little proud or, what's the word, vindicated, but I didn't. It made no difference whatever. It was still way short of what it would cost to get to Massachusetts and live there and pay all the costs, and anyhow I wasn't going there. I was supposed to answer within ten days, but I just stuck the letter into the drawer of the desk and forgot about it. I mean I really did forget about it. It just didn't mean anything.

Jason wanted to go to a show on Friday night, but I said I was doing something with my parents, and I told them I was going to the show with Jason. I was doing a lot of lying like that. Just dumb lies that didn't hurt anybody or make any big difference; it was easier to tell lies about

7 **furrow** ['fʌrəʊ] a long, narrow trench made in the ground by a plough – 25 **vindicated** proved to be right – 26 **it was way short of ...** it was by far not enough ...

things than to tell the truth. If I told Jason I didn't want to go to a show, he would have argued. If I told either him or my parents that I was going to hear this concert at a church, they would have thought it was a funny thing to do, and I was sick and tired of always being the only person who ever did funny things. And they might have noticed the sign then and seen Natalie's name, and that was none of their business. And Jason might even have come with me, because he was so bored he'd do almost anything so long as there was somebody to do it with. So it was a lot easier to lie about it. If you lied about enough things, then everybody else got involved in the fog, too, and they couldn't see you, or touch you at all.

I felt very peculiar going there, Friday night. It was late April and one of the first warm nights, warm and windy, all the flowers out in the gardens, and clouds blowing across the stars. Walking to the church I felt dizzy. You know that feeling where you seem to have done all this before? Well, this was just the opposite. It was as if I'd never seen those streets before, though I walked them twice a day five days a week. Everything was different. I felt like a stranger, in the late evening in a strange city. It was frightening, but I liked it too, in a way. I thought, what if none of the people in the houses I passed and the cars passing me were speaking English, what if they were all speaking some language I didn't know, and this was really a foreign city I had never seen before, and I only thought I'd lived here all my life because I was going crazy.

I looked at things, the trees, the houses, the way a tourist would, and it really seemed to be true, I'd never seen them before. The wind kept blowing in my face.

When I got to the church and other people were going in, I felt very nervous and irritable. I sort of crept in. I would have gone on all fours if I could have so as to be less visible. It was a big old church, mostly wood, hollow and dark and high inside. Since I'd never been in it, it was easy to keep up the feeling of being a total stranger, a foreigner. There were quite a lot of people there and more coming in, but I didn't know any of them. I didn't know where Natalie would sit, probably down in front, so I took a seat at the end of a pew in the last row, clear across the church from where the people came in, behind a pillar, as inconspicuous a place as I could find. I didn't want to see or be seen. I wanted to be alone. The

10 **involved** included – 35 **pillar** tall, narrow structure supporting part of a building – **inconspicuous** [ˌɪnkənˈspɪkjʊəs] not noticeable

only people I saw that I knew even by sight were two girls from school, maybe friends of Natalie's. The church got quite full, but being in a church nobody talked loud, and the sound of them talking was like water on the beach, a big soft noise, not English, not anything. I sat there reading the mimeographed programme and feeling dizzy and unearthly – detached, completely detached.

The songs were the next to last thing on the programme. The orchestra was pretty good, I guess; I didn't listen hard, I kept floating; but I sort of vaguely enjoyed the music, because it let me float. There was an intermission, but I stayed in my seat. Then finally the singer stood up, down in front. The accompaniment was a string quartet, and Natalie was playing the viola part. I hadn't expected that. I saw her sitting there next to a big middle-aged man cellist; he hid most of her, I could just see her hair looking sleek and jet black in the lights. Then I ducked down again. The conductor, who was the chatty type, went on for a while about Music in Our City and about this promising young musician and composer of eighteen, and finally shut up, and the music began.

The singer was good. She was just somebody who sang at the church, I guess, but she had a strong voice, and she understood the words and the music. The first song was 'Love and Friendship', a simple poem about how love is like the wild rose but friendship is the holly tree. It had a good tune, and you could tell the audience thought it was very pretty. They applauded hard at the end. Natalie sat there and scowled and didn't look up. They weren't supposed to applaud until all three songs were sung. The singer looked embarrassed and half bowed, and the audience finally got the idea and shut up. Then she sang the second one. Emily Brontë wrote the words when she was twenty-two.

Riches I hold in light esteem
And Love I laugh to scorn
And lust of Fame was but a dream
That vanished with the morn –

5 **mimeographed** ['mɪmɪəgræft] *(A.E.)* duplicated – 6 **detached** disconnected – 8 **to float** *here:* to feel as if moving slowly on water – 10 **intermission** a break between two parts of a concert, etc. – 28 **esteem** [-'-] appreciation – 31 **to vanish** ['vænɪʃ] to disappear – **morn** *(poetic)* morning

And if I pray, the only prayer
That moves my lips for me
Is – 'Leave the heart that now I bear
And give me liberty.'

Yes, as my swift days near their goal
'Tis all that I implore –
Through life and death, a chainless soul
With courage to endure!

The violins and the cello played long notes softly in a kind of shivering drone, and there was a double tune, the singer and the viola, singing with and against each other. A hard, reaching, grieving tune. And it broke through, on those last four words, and stopped.

The audience didn't applaud. Maybe they didn't know it was over, maybe they didn't like it, maybe it scared them. The whole place was perfectly silent. Then they did the third song, 'Mild the mist upon the hill', very softly. I began crying, and I couldn't stop when it was over and they were clapping and Natalie had to stand up and take bows. I got up and blundered around the back of the pews, by feel mostly because I couldn't see for crying, and got out of the church into the night.

I started to walk up towards the Park. The street lamps were big blobs of light with rainbow haloes and the wind was cold on the tears on my face. My head was hot and light and ringing with the singer's voice. I didn't feel the pavement under my feet, and if I passed anyone I never saw them. And I didn't care if they saw me walking on the street crying.

There was a glory in it. It was too much for me to take, everything coming together at once, but there was a glory in it. And that was partly love. I mean real love. In the song I had seen Natalie whole the way she really was, and I loved her. It was not an emotion or a desire, it was a confirmation, it was a glory, like seeing the stars. To know that she could do that, that she could make a song that made people be still and listen, and made me cry, to know that that was Natalie, it really was, it was her, herself, the truth.

3 **to bear** to have, to carry; to endure – 5 **swift** fast – 6 **to implore** [ɪm'plɔ:] to beg desperately – 8 **to endure** [ɪn'djʊə] to patiently suffer through a difficult situation, hard life, etc. – 11 **a grieving tune** a sad melody – 21 **halo** ['heɪləʊ] a round disc of light, usu. around the head of a saint

But there was so much pain in it, and I couldn't handle it.

After a couple of blocks my tears dried up. I walked on, but by the time I got to the edge of the Park I was so tired I turned around and headed for home. It was about fifteen blocks, and as I walked I wasn't thinking or feeling anything that I can remember. I just walked in the night, and I could have been doing it forever and gone on doing it forever. Only the sense of strangeness was gone. Everything was familiar, the whole world, the stars even, I was at home. Now and then there was the smell of fresh earth or flowers from a dark garden. I remember that.

I came to our street and turned down it. Just as I came towards the Fields' house their car pulled up in front of it, and Mr and Mrs Field and Natalie and another young woman got out. They were all talking. I stopped short and just stood. I was between street lights, and it's very strange that Natalie could see me off there in the dark. But she came straight towards me. I stood there.

'Owen?'

I said, 'Yeah, hi.'

'I saw you at the concert.'

'Yeah. I heard you,' I said, and gave a sort of laugh.

She was carrying her viola case. She had on a long dress, her hair still looked very black and smooth, and her face was bright. Playing her music, and then I suppose a reception afterwards with people congratulating her, had got her keyed up, tense; her eyes looked big.

'You left after my songs.'

'Yeah. Is that when you saw me?'

'I saw you earlier. At the back. I was looking for you.'

'You thought I'd be there?'

'I hoped you would. No. I thought you would.'

Her father called her from the front steps: 'Natalie!'

'Is he proud of you?' I asked.

She nodded.

'I have to go in,' she said. 'My sister came for the concert. Do you want to come in?'

'I can't.'

I meant I couldn't, not that anybody was preventing me.

'Will you come tomorrow night?' she said in a sudden voice, fiercely.

I said, 'All right.'

'I want to see you,' she said in the same way. Then she turned around and went to the house and went in, and I walked on past and came home.

My father was watching TV and my mother was sitting with him doing crewelwork. She said, 'Short movie?' and I said it was, and she said, 'Did you enjoy it? What was it?' and I said, 'Oh, I don't know,' and went upstairs, because I'd walked right out of the night wind back into the fog. And I couldn't talk in the fog, I couldn't say anything true.

It was not my parents' fault. If this seems to be one of those books about how everything is the older generation's fault, and even some psychologists have written books like that by the way, then I haven't said it right. It wasn't their fault. All right, so they lived partly in the fog all the time, and accepted a lot of lies without trying to get at the truth – so what? Who doesn't? It doesn't mean they liked it, any better than I did. It doesn't mean they were strong. It means just the opposite.

I went over to Natalie's the next night. It was like the first time: Mrs Field let me in, and Natalie was practising. I waited in the dark hall, and the music stopped, and she came down the stairs. She said, 'Let's go for a walk.'

'It's raining.'

'I don't care,' she said. 'I want to get out.'

She put on her coat and we started up the street towards the Park. She still had that tense, high-flying look. It was going to take her a while to come back down.

'What's been happening with you?' she said after we'd gone half a block.

'Nothing much.'

'Have you heard from any of the colleges?'

'Yeah, one.'

'Which one?'

'M.I.T.'

'What did they say?'

'Oh, they'll let me in.'

'No money?'

'Yeah, tuition.'

'Full tuition?'

'Yeah, right.'

'Wow. That's great! So what did you decide?'

8 **psychologist** [saɪˈkɒlədʒɪst]

'Nothing.'

'You waiting to hear from the others?'

'No.'

'What do you mean?'

'Oh, I'm going to State, I guess.'

'State? What for?'

'To get a college degree.'

'But why there? You wanted to work with that fellow at M.I.T.'

'First-year students don't go and "work with" Nobel Prize winners.'

'They don't stay first-year students either, do they?'

'Yeah, well, I decided not to.'

'I thought you said you didn't decide anything.'

'There isn't anything to decide.'

She shoved her hands in her coat pockets and hunched her head over and strode along clumping her heels. She looked mad. But after about a block she said, 'Owen.'

'Yeah.'

'I am really confused.'

'What about?'

I don't know how she could go on, I was answering her in such a cold, dumb, uninterested tone. But she went on.

'About Jade Beach and all that.'

'Oh, yeah. Well, that's all right.'

I didn't want to talk about it. It loomed up out of the fog much too big and solid and hard. I wanted to turn away and not look at it.

'I've been thinking about it a lot,' she said. 'See, I thought I had all that figured out. At least for a while. For the next couple of years anyhow. The way I figured, I didn't want to get really involved with anybody. Falling in love or love affairs or marrying or anything like that. I'm pretty young, and there's all these things I have to do. That sounds stupid but it's the truth. If I could take sex lightly the way a lot of people do, that would be fine, but I don't think I can. I can't take anything lightly. Well, see, what was so beautiful was that we got to be friends. There's the kind of love that's lovers, and the kind of love that's friends. And I really thought it was that way. I thought we'd really made it, and everybody's wrong when they say men and women can't be friends. But I guess they're right. I was … too theoretical …'

15 **to stride (strode, stridden)** to walk with long steps – 24 **to loom** to appear as a problem or anything frightening

'I don't know,' I said. I didn't want to say anything more, but it got dragged up out of me. 'I think you were right, actually. I was pushing the sex stuff in where it didn't belong.'

'Yeah, but it does belong,' she said in this defeated, morose voice. And then in the fierce voice, 'You can't just tell sex to go away and come back in two years because I'm busy just now!'

We went on another block. The rain was fine and misty so that you hardly felt it on your face, but it was beginning to drip down the back of my neck.

'The first fellow I went out with,' she said, 'I was sixteen and he was eighteen; he was an oboist, oboists are all crazy. He had a car and he kept parking it in places with a nice view and then, you know, sort of launching himself onto me. And he started saying, "This is bigger than either of us, Natalie!" And it made me mad and I finally said, "Well it may be bigger than you, but it isn't bigger than me!" That sort of finished that. He was a jerk anyhow. So was I. But anyhow. Now I know what he meant.'

After a while she went on, 'But all the same ...'

'What?'

'It doesn't belong. Does it?'

'What?'

'With you and me. It just doesn't work. Does it?'

'No,' I said.

She got mad then. She stopped walking and looked at me with that scowl. 'You say yes, you say no, you say there isn't anything to decide – Well, there is! And did I decide right or didn't I? *I* don't know! Why do I have to make the decision? If we're friends – and that's the whole point of it, can we be friends – then we make the decisions together – don't we?'

'O.K. We did.'

'Then why are you mad at me?'

We were standing there under a big horse chestnut tree. It was dark under the branches and they kept most of the rain off. Some of the flowers shone like candles in the streetlight, above us. Natalie's coat and hair were all like shadows, all I could see of her was her face and eyes.

4 **morose** [məˈrəʊs] miserable, bad-tempered – 13 **to launch** [lɔ:ntʃ] to rush forward – 25 **scowl** [skaʊl] a look of anger – 32 **horse chestnut** [ˈtʃesnʌt] *Roßkastanie*

'I'm not,' I said. It was like the ground was shifting under me, the world reorganizing itself, an earthquake, nothing to hold on to. 'I'm really mixed-up. It's just that. I can't make sense out of anything. I can't handle it.'

'Why not, Owen? What's wrong?'

'I don't know,' I said, and I put my hands on her shoulders, and she came up close and held me around the ribs.

'I get scared,' I said.

She said, 'What of?' into my coat.

'Being alive.'

She held on to me and I held on to her.

'I don't know what to do,' I said. 'See, I'm supposed to go on living all these years and I don't know how.'

'You mean you don't know why?'

'I guess so.'

'But, for this,' she said, holding on. 'For this. For you, for the stuff you have to do, for time to think, for time to hear the music. You know how, Owen. Only you listen to the people who don't!'

'Yeah, I guess so,' I said. I was shaking. She said, 'It's cold. Let's go home and make some weird tea. I've got some Chinese tea that's supposed to be very calming and aids longevity.'

'Longevity is just what I need right now.'

We started back. I don't think we said anything much going back or while we were standing around in the kitchen waiting for the water to boil. We took the teapot and cups up to the practice room and sat on the oriental rug. That Chinese herb tea tasted really vile. It left your mouth feeling scoured out, but that was kind of pleasant once you got used to it. I was still feeling shaken up, but I was getting used to that, too.

'Did you ever finish the Thorn Quintet?' I said.

Actually it had only been eight weeks since I had seen her, but it seemed like eight years, and we were in a whole new place.

'Not yet. The slow movement's done, and I have the idea for the last movement.'

'Listen, Nat. Your stuff last night, the songs, you know. It made me cry. The second one.'

'I know. That's why I had to talk to you again. I mean, because I knew we could. I mean, because …'

21 **longevity** [lɒn'dʒevɪtɪ] long life – 26 **vile** nasty, horrible – 27 **scoured out** ['skaʊəd] scrubbed out

'Because that's the way you really talk. The rest is just words.'

She looked at me straight on and she said, 'Owen, you are the neatest person I ever knew. Nobody else understands that. I don't even know any other musicians who understand that. I can't really say anything. I can't even really be anything. Except in music. Maybe later. Maybe when I get good at music, maybe when I learn how to do that, then I'll be able to do some of the rest, too. Maybe I'll even become a human being. But you *are* one.'

'I'm an ape,' I said. 'Trying to do the human act.'

'You're good at it,' she said, 'the best I ever knew.'

I lay down on the rug on my stomach and looked down into my cup of tea. It was a sort of murky yellow brown, with bits of Chinese sediment floating around in it.

'If this stuff is really calming,' I said, 'I wonder if it works on the central nervous system, or the cerebrum, or the cerebellum, or where.'

'It tastes like steel wool pads. I wonder if they're calming.'

'I don't know, I never ate one.'

'For breakfast, with milk and sugar.'

'Five thousand per cent of the minimum daily adult iron requirement.'

She laughed and wiped her eyes. 'I wish I could talk,' she said, 'I wish I was like you.'

'What did I ever say?'

'I can't tell you because I can't talk. I can play it, though.'

'I want to hear it.'

She got up and went to the piano and played some music I had never heard before.

When it was done I said, 'Is it Thorn?' and she nodded.

'See, if I could just live there,' I said, 'everything would be duck soup.'

'You do live there. That's where you live.'

'Alone?'

'Maybe.'

'I don't want to be alone. I'm tired of myself.'

'Well, you could let visitors come. In small boats.'

'I don't want to play king of the castle any more. I want to live with

12 **murky** not clear – 16 **steel wool** a mass of fine steel threads woven together and used for cleaning metal surfaces – 29 **duck soup** *(sl.)* s.th. easy to do

other people, Nat. I used to think other people don't matter, but they do. You can't hack it all by yourself.'

'Is that why you're going to State?'

'I guess so.'

'But you said last winter that your problem at school was the way things are set up there, to level everybody down so that nobody's anybody. Won't State be just like that only bigger?'

'The entire world is like school, only bigger.'

'No it isn't.' She looked stubborn, and played some very ugly chords very softly on the piano. 'School is where you can't decide anything yet. The rest of the world is where you have to. You aren't going to, you know, decide never to decide anything, be a groupie, are you?'

'But see, I'm so sick of going against the others, being different. It gets you nowhere. If I do like the others do –'

She went BRWHANNGGG! on the piano keys.

'The others are all doing like the other others, so that they can all get along together and not be alone,' I said. 'Man is a social species. So why the hell can't I?'

'Because you aren't any good at it,' she said.

'So what do I do? Go back to Thorn and be a crazy hermit the rest of my life writing dumb stuff nobody reads?'

'No. You go to M.I.T. and show them how good you are.'

'It costs too much.'

BRRWWWHAANNNGGG!

'They give him three thousand dollars and he *complains*,' she said.

'It's going to cost like sixteen or twenty thousand to go there just the first four years.'

'Borrow it. Steal it. Sell your stupid car!'

'I already wrecked it,' I said, and I began to laugh.

'Wrecked it? The car? In the accident?'

'A write-off,' I said, laughing like crazy. She began laughing, too. I have no idea why we were laughing. It was all of a sudden funny. The whole thing. Everything had been so out of proportion, and all of a sudden it was like I was in proportion, and could see it.

'My father got practically the whole value of it in insurance,' I said. 'Cash.'

2 **to hack** *(coll.)* to cope with successfully, to manage – 12 **groupie** *here:* opposite of "individualist" – 20 **hermit** ['hɜːmɪt] a person who lives in complete isolation

'Well then!'

'Well then.'

'There's your first year. You worry about the next year next year.'

'Gorillas build new nests every night,' I said. 'They sleep in nests, up in trees. They build really lousy ones, very sloppy. They have to build new ones every night, because they keep moving on, and besides they foul up the old ones with banana peels and other effluvia. The rule for primates, maybe, is to keep moving on and building nests, one at a time, until they learn to do it right. Or to throw out the banana peels at least.'

Natalie was still sitting at the piano, and she played about six seconds of a thing by Chopin that she had been studying back in December, the Revolutionary Etude. She said, 'I wish I understood ...'

I got up off the floor and sat down by her on the piano bench and played some nothing with both hands. 'See, I don't understand how to play the piano. But when you play it, I hear the music.'

She looked at me and I looked at her, and we kissed each other on the mouth. But modestly: six seconds at the maximum.

There is more, of course, but that seems to be all of this thing I wanted to tell. The 'more' is just what happened next and keeps on happening – each day's new gorilla nest.

I got the scholarship thing out of my desk drawer next day and showed it to my parents, and said that with the car insurance money I could get started at M.I.T. My mother began to get very upset, really angry, as if I was pulling a dirty trick on her. I don't know if I could have handled that, but my father came in on my side. This is what you always forget, you think you know what to expect but you don't; what you expect is what doesn't happen and what you don't expect is what does. My father said that if I worked each summer and kept getting tuition scholarships he would pay the rest. My mother felt really betrayed and refused to go along with the plan gracefully. But she had to go along ungracefully, because despite the fact that she runs our household, she has always played this game that the man is the one who makes the decisions, and so she has cut herself out from decision-making, unless the decisions are not made but just happen, which is

7 **effluvia** [ɪ'flu:vjə] waste, garbage – 29 **to betray s.o.** to be disloyal to s.o. – 30 **graceful** kind and pleasant; opposite of "sullen"

how she prefers it to be. She left herself no option but resentment. That would have been awfully hard to take, if I hadn't had my father backing me up. As it was, it was painful, but endurable. My mother is actually too good-natured to keep on resenting week after week. She began forgetting to resent by about the middle of May. A couple of weeks after that she bought me some ties, very tasteful dark stripes, because she has this conviction that Eastern College Men wear ties to class.

I got back to work at school and finished up with all top marks. If you are going to be an egghead, you might as well be a hardboiled one. I have a job this summer as a starting lab technician at Bico Industries.

Natalie and I saw each other several times a week in May and June. It was difficult sometimes, because we did not always manage to stick to the six-second maximum. As she said, neither of us are good at taking things lightly. We had several sort of quarrels, because we would both be somewhat frustrated, and take it out on the other. But they lasted only about five minutes, because we were basically certain that we couldn't make any commitment yet, and that sex was no good to us without a commitment, but that we were no good without love. So the best we could do was just go on as we were, together. It was a very good best.

She left for Tanglewood the last week in June. She went by train. I saw her off, which was embarrassing since her parents were seeing her off too. But I felt I had the right, despite the fact that Mr Field sill made me feel about as welcome as a tarantula. I just sort of stood around, there on the railway platform. Now and then Mrs Field stood back slightly, so that I was partially included and could see Natalie. She had her viola case in one hand and her violin case in the other and a back-pack, so she wasn't very mobile. At the steps up to her carriage, she kissed her mother and father. She didn't kiss me. She looked at me. She said, 'See you in the East, a year from September, Owen.'

'Or in Thorn, permanently,' I said.

She waved through the dirty window from her seat as the train started up. I did not do the ape act. I stood there and did the human act as well as possible.

1 **option** alternative – **but** *here:* except – **resentment** bitterness – 9 **egghead** *(sl.)* an intellectual – 15 **to take it out on s.o.** to attack s.o. because one feels frustrated or angry – 17 **to make a commitment** *here:* to enter a permanent relationship

Additional Texts

1. American Education

The U.S. Constitution leaves all educational matters to the individual states. There are, then, 50 different educational systems operating independently of one another. Each of the states sets its own broad standards and guidelines. The actual control of the public school – what is taught when to whom by whom – is in the hands of the local communities. These local divisions are called "school districts", and there are about 16,000 of these across the country. Each district is controlled by a school board whose members are elected by the citizens in each district. Local taxes also pay for a significant part of public school education, about 43 % nationwide (with only around 6 % coming from federal sources, and the rest from the state governments). Moreover, the local communities actually vote as to whether they wish to pay more taxes for their schools or not.

This system of local control and financing has very important effects on the high schools in three ways. First, with each school district hiring and firing its own teachers and setting its own curriculum, and with local citizens electing the school boards and paying part of the bill, high schools very much reflect the interests, wishes, and needs of each community. Second, there tend to be great differences in quality among individual schools, with wealthier districts able or willing to pay more for their schools. And finally, with 16,000 different school districts, there is an enormous variety among individual high schools. There are large, inner-city schools sometimes having up to 4,000 students, and offering several hundred different courses, and there are small rural schools where everyone knows each other. There are excellent academic programs and poor ones, conservative teaching staffs and extremely liberal ones. This variety is not only normal, it's the norm. Somewhere in America, everything is being taught in high schools, from Arabic to water-skiing and from Yiddish to yoga.

1 **Constitution** the basic law of a country which lays down how the political powers are to be separated, etc. – 10 **federal** coming not from the state governments, but from the central government in Washington – 17 **bill** *here:* expenses – 26 **teaching staff** all the teachers at a particular school

The United States Educational Structure

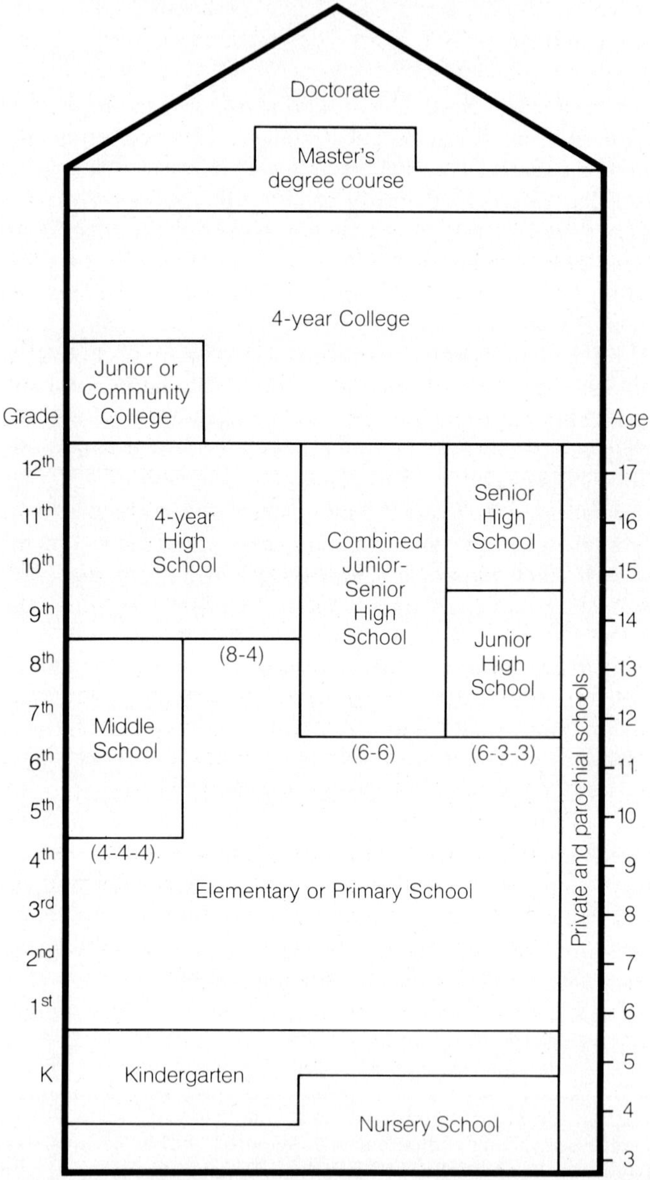

These differences are fundamental ones. There are, however, enough similarities among all the different high schools to allow some generalizations to be made. Most children attend the public high schools, some 88% (with the rest attending church-related or purely private ones). Almost all states require children to stay in school until they are at least 16 years old. Most students finish high school when they're 18, although finishing at 16 or 17 is not uncommon. Students go to school five days a week, usually starting around 8 and finishing classes in mid-afternoon. There is usually a free week or so around Christmas as well as other public holidays determined by each state, and district. The long summer vacation period – from sometime in June until early in September – reflects America's agricultural heritage when children were needed to work on the farms.

While students are often together in some classes, each generally follows a pre-university program of academic studies, or a program which stresses vocational, job-related skills, or a combination of both. All students are required to take certain basic courses, and a number of courses in different academic areas. Often, students are allowed to choose among several courses in one area. For example, among foreign languages they might choose Spanish (the most popular language today), or among vocational subjects, computers or automotive repair. No high school allows its students to take whatever they want, and a variety of tests or examinations is expected for each subject. Students are given grades on an A (high) to E or F (low) basis. When a student has taken an established number of courses in a set number of areas and done well enough in each, he or she can graduate.

Like schools in all English-speaking countries, American high schools also emphasize social and sports activities. Here, too, there is enormous variety. There are school orchestras, bands and choirs. There are Latin or Russian clubs, school newspapers, computer or horse-riding clubs, drama, chess, amateur radio, rodeo, or what have you. Almost all schools have their own swimming pools, gymnasiums, and athletic fields (or even stadiums) which they share with the community. Some sports such as football, basketball, baseball, swimming, wrestling, or track and field have school teams which compete against other schools. These and other sports are also played just for fun. High school students

41 **heritage** ['herɪtɪdʒ] history and tradition – 64 **track and field** athletic activities which take place on a running track or sports field (e.g. running, jumping)

are commonly also involved in community service projects or in raising money, for example, to help a choir or a debating club to take a trip somewhere. Almost all so-called extracurricular activities take place after classes have finished. As a result, many students don't return home until early evening. One might think that with courses and extracurricular activities (and homework) little time would be available for anything else. Nonetheless, about 75% of all high school seniors (i.e. those in the 12th grade) in the U.S. have part-time jobs during the school week.

Almost all high schools provide both personal and guidance counseling for their students. Should a student, for example, have a personal problem (e.g. "my parents are getting divorced, and ...") he or she can talk with someone who has been professionally trained to help people. Similarly, trained guidance counselors help students to decide which courses to take, which jobs, careers or professions they might be interested in, and importantly, which colleges and universities provide financial aid, scholarships, and work-study programs.

Anyone who successfully finishes high school is given a piece of paper called a diploma (those who don't get a diploma – even if they stay in school until they can legally leave – are known as "dropouts"). The diploma, however, is not a ticket that allows you to enter a university. Each university and college sets its own admissions requirements, and competition for the better universities is intense. One of the best universities, Stanford University in California, only accepts about 16% of all the qualified students who apply each year. Most universities and colleges require applicants to take a standardized test, the best known being the SAT, or Scholastic Aptitude Test. Each year some 2 million high school students take this test on specific dates and at locations throughout the nation. The test is not "official" or controlled by any governmental group or agency. But those high school students who went to the better high schools, who studied harder and took the harder courses, usually do better and can get into the better universities than those who did only what they had to, or spent more time on merrymaking than mathematics.

Some colleges and universities are virtually free to residents of the state, with only token academic fees. Thus tuition at Oregon State

100 **residents** people who live in a particular city or state – 101 **token** *(adj.) here:* very small, unimportant

University was $1,833 in 1992. Others can be quite expensive, costing as much as $17,000 or more a year. For example, tuition was $16,900 at M.I.T. in 1992. At the same time, however, there are a great many scholarships, financial aid programs, and work opportunities: you do not need to be rich to attend the best universities! Some 40% of all students at Harvard University, for instance, receive scholarships, and a great many students work at part-time jobs, "on campus" or off. Today, about two-thirds of all university students in the U.S. pay for their own university education, not their parents.

Like a professional football team that is always looking for talent, the best universities are always trying to find the best students. If you are a good student, you can almost always find a scholarship, a federal or state loan program, or a work-study arrangement which will help you to help yourself. It's not an easy life, working and studying at the same time.

Special contribution by Douglas K. Stevenson

2. A Game Called Dating

The game is described as dating; boys take out girls, girls have to be asked, boys have to ask, both must dress correctly according to the adolescent styles of the moment, the date must be conducted in some way so that it can be known to the rest of the group – otherwise it doesn't count. The long association of courtship and costume through the ages rather obscures the issue here. Because dating and dressing are so closely associated, the assumption is that it is courtship. But men have worn war-paint to impress their enemies or their male comrades, and women have done battle against their own sex in pearls and ostrich-feathers, before now. The clothes, the flowers, the dancing, are all part of the game, but they are to be equated neither with courtship nor with behaviour that is primarily sexual, although the pattern of dating does

108 **on campus** on the university grounds – 114 **loan** sum of money you can borrow

3 **adolescent styles** [ˌædəʊ'lesnt] styles favoured by teenagers (i.e. adolescents) – 5 **courtship** the time during which a man pays a lot of attention to a woman because he wants to marry her – 6 **issue** point, subject talked about – 9 **ostrich** ['ɒstrɪtʃ] a very large bird of South Africa *(Vogel Strauß)* – 11 **to equate s.th. with s.th.** [ɪ'kweɪt] to say that s.th is equal to s.th. else – 12 **pattern** characteristic way in which s.th. is done

in the end have a profound effect on the later relationships of men and women in America.

That dating is primarily a competitive game in which publicly affirmed popularity is the prize can be illustrated by considering the behaviour of those who do not date, but withdraw, sometimes quite early in adolescence, to "going steady." For here we find two groups: young people whose stirring sexuality has been genuinely aroused so that they may be said to be "in love" with each other, and who find the game of dating meaningless because they prefer each other's company; and young people who, without being in love, depend on each other for protection, the unpopular girl and the unpopular boy, concealing their failure in the popularity game by pretending to prefer each other. Outside the dating group are much larger peripheral groups: girls and boys who are so physically immature and dysplastic that they feel disqualified for this game where mimic physical readiness for sex is expected; girls and boys who lack the money and the clothes; girls and boys who have such a deep interest in something else that it protects them from wanting to spend their time in a game that is to them irrelevant. But for those who are allowed to play, the deep fear of deviance – natural offspring of our hurriedly assembled and slightly learned cultural patterns – keeps them in the game, demonstrating that they are successful in the way in which their adolescent social world, and every magazine they pick up, and their parents' expectation, decrees that they shall be.

But what effect on the actual sex behaviour of Americans does the dating pattern have? In the first place, it defines the relationship between a male and a female as situational. You "have a date," you "go out with a date," you "groan because there isn't a decent date in town." A situation defined as containing a girl – or boy – of the right social background, the right degree of popularity, a little higher than your own, is what one sighs for, or boasts about. Now superficially this may not look very different from the "girl in a punt" of English undergraduate day-dreams, or the "girl and a full moon" recurrent in romantic

19 **to arouse** to awaken – 23 **to conceal s.th.** to keep s.th. a secret – 26 **dysplastic** *(formal) here:* unable to act – 27 **mimic** simulated, acted – 31 **fear of deviance** ['di:vjəns] fear of behaving differently from what people consider normal or acceptable – 32 **offspring** *here:* result – 35 **to decree** to rule – 39 **to groan** to give a sound of pain – **decent** ['di:snt] of acceptable quality – 42 **to boast about s.th.** to speak very proudly about s.th. – 43 **punt** a long boat with a flat bottom *(Stechkahn)* – **undergraduate** a college or university student who has not yet received a degree – 44 **recurrent** [rɪ'kʌrənt] which recurs, i.e. is repeated or happens again

song. But the boy who longs for a date is not longing for a girl. He is longing to be in a situation, mainly public, where he will be seen by others to have a girl, and the right kind of girl, who dresses well and pays attention. He takes her out as he takes out his new car, but more impersonally, because the car is his for good but the girl is his only for the evening.

From *Male and Female* by Margaret Mead, New York: William Morrow & Company, 1949, pp. 285–287.

3. The Stage of Adolescing

As technological advances put more and more time between early school life and the young person's final access to specialized work, the stage of adolescing becomes an even more marked and conscious period and, as it has always been in some cultures in some periods, almost a way of life between childhood and adulthood. Thus in the later school years young people, beset with the physiological revolution of their genital maturation and the uncertainty of the adult roles ahead, seem much concerned with faddish attempts at establishing an adolescent subculture with what looks like a final rather than a transitory or, in fact, initial identity formation. They are sometimes morbidly, often curiously, preoccupied with what they appear to be in the eyes of others as compared with what they feel they are, and with the question of how to connect the roles and skills cultivated earlier with the ideal prototypes of the day. In their search for a new sense of continuity and sameness, which must now include sexual maturity, some adolescents have to come to grips again with crises of earlier years before they can install lasting idols and ideals as guardians of a final identity. [...]

The danger of this stage is role confusion. Where this is based on a

45 **to long for s.th.** to want s.th. very much – 49 **for good** for ever
6 **to beset (beset, beset)** to trouble – 7 **maturation** the process of becoming mature, i.e. of reaching a state of complete development – 8 **concerned with s.th.** giving much attention to s.th. – **attempt** the act of trying to do s.th. – **faddish attempts** *here:* attempts lasting for a very short time – 9 **transitory** ['trænsɪtərɪ] passing, lasting only for a short time – 16 **to come to grips with s.th.** to deal with s.th. (usually a problem) – 17 **to install** to establish

strong previous doubt as to one's sexual identity, delinquent and outright psychotic episodes are not uncommon. If diagnosed and treated correctly, these incidents do not have the same fatal significance which they have at other ages. In most instances, however, it is the inability to settle on an occupational identity which disturbs individual young people. To keep themselves together they temporarily overidentify, to the point of apparent complete loss of identity, with the heroes of cliques and crowds. This initiates the stage of "falling in love," which is by no means entirely, or even primarily, a sexual matter – except where the *mores* demand it. To a considerable extent adolescent love is an attempt to arrive at a definition of one's identity by projecting one's diffused ego-image on another and by seeing it thus reflected and gradually clarified. This is why so much of young love is conversation.

Young people can also be remarkably clannish, and cruel in their exclusion of all those who are "different," in skin colour or cultural background, in tastes and gifts, and often in such petty aspects of dress and gesture as have been temporarily selected as *the* signs of an in-grouper or out-grouper. It is important to understand (which does not mean condone or participate in) such intolerance as a defence against a sense of identity confusion. For adolescents not only help one another temporarily through much discomfort by forming cliques and by stereotyping themselves, their ideals, and their enemies; they also perversely test each other's capacity to pledge fidelity. The readiness for such testing also explains the appeal which simple and cruel totalitarian doctrines have on the minds of the youth of such countries and classes as have lost or are losing their group identities (feudal, agrarian, tribal, national) and face world-wide industrialization, emancipation, and wider communication.

From *Identity, Youth and Crisis* by Erik H. Erikson, New York: W. W. Norton, 1968, pp. 128, 253–254.

19 **outright** open, direct – 28 **mores** ['mɔːreɪz] the customs and conventions of a particular group or society – **extent** degree – 34 **petty** small, unimportant – 37 **to condone** [kən'dəʊn] to accept or seem to accept s.th. although one knows it is morally wrong – 41 **to pledge s.th.** to promise solemnly to do s.th. – 42 **appeal** attraction

4. The Role of the Peer-group

[...] the adults are anxious that the child succeed in the peer-group and therefore are concerned with his "adjustment." They, too, tend to ignore and even suppress invisible differences between their child and the children of others. Such differences might cast doubt on their own adjustment, their own correct tuning to the signals concerning child rearing.

The majority of children learn very fast under these conditions; the same adult authorities who patronize children's intellects (and therefore slow them down) are perhaps not sufficiently impressed with how poised in many social situations modern other-directed children are. These children are not shy, either with adults or with the opposite sex whom they have accompanied to proms and parties and seen daily in and out of school. This adaptability, moreover, prepares the child for a type of social mobility somewhat different from the social-climbing experiences of the parvenu in an inner-directed environment. The latter only rarely acquired the intellectual and social graces of his new associates – or he ridiculously accentuated them. He either kept his rough and lowly manners or painfully tried to learn new ones as he moved up; in either case the standard, limited code of conduct expected of him was unequivocal. In contrast with this the other-directed child is able to move among new associates with an almost automatic adjustment to the subtlest insignia of status.

Bearing in mind these positive achievements of other-directed sociability, let us turn our attention from what the peer-group teaches and evokes to what it represses. Today six-year-olds and up have a phrase – "he [or she] thinks he's *big*" (or "he thinks he's *something*") – which

peer-group a group of people of about the same age, background, social standing etc., sharing the same values. People's behaviour may be influenced by their association with their peer-group (= "peer pressure") – 2 **adjustment** the act of adapting to a situation – 4 **to cast doubt on s.th.** to cause people to be uncertain about s.th. – 10 **poised** calm and confident – **other-directed children** children who are guided by a set of values derived from outward influences rather than from within (opposite of "inner-directed") – 12 **prom** *(A.E.)* a ball held for a high school class at the end of the academic year – 15 **parvenu** ['pɑ:vənju:] a person who has suddenly risen to a higher social status without having the appropriate cultural background – 19 **code of conduct** ['kɒndʌkt] the way s.o. is expected to behave in society – 20 **unequivocal** [ˌʌnɪ'kwɪvəkl] absolutely clear – 25 **to evoke** [ɪ'vəʊk] to bring to mind symbolizes the role of the peer-group in the creation of other-directed types. The effort is to cut everyone down to size who stands up or stands out in any direction. Beginning with the very young and going on from there, overt vanity is treated as one of the worst offenses, as perhaps dishonesty would have been in an earlier day. Being high-hat is forbidden.

Temper, manifest jealousy, moodiness – these, too, are offenses in the code of the peer-group. All knobby or idiosyncratic qualities and vices are more or less eliminated or repressed.

From *The Lonely Crowd – A Study of the Changing American Character* by David Riesman with Nathan Glazer and Reuel Denney, New Haven, Conn.: Yale University Press, 1961, pp. 71–72.

5. Women in the Musical World

Women, then, were only allowed to enter the public musical world when they could not be replaced by men. They have gradually become tolerated – even if always with misgivings – in the reproductive sphere, although a few instruments such as the brass and percussion have largely remained the prerogative of men. However, in the productive sphere – that of composition – women have never been encouraged; on the contrary, music academies were closed to them for centuries, their compositions were ignored, ridiculed or, even worse, given "feminine" attributes such as "insipid", "pretty", "lacking in scope" etc.

A comparison with other art forms shows that this disregard for female creativity was not unique. Women have always only been allowed a first foothold in those areas where creativity was considered to be of secondary importance. For example, it was through needlework and the applied arts that women were first able to enter the fine arts.

30 **overt** ['əʊvɜ:t] open – 34 **knobby** ['nɒbɪ] *here:* having distinctive and very noticeable individual traits – **idiosyncratic** [ɪdɪəsɪŋ'krætɪk] characteristic of an individual – **vice** immoral or criminal behaviour or inclinations
3 **misgivings** negative feelings, resentment – **sphere** [sfɪə] area – 4 **brass** instruments like trumpets, saxophones, etc. – **percussion** instruments like drums, gongs, etc. – 5 **prerogative** [-'---] privilege – 9 **insipid** boring – **lacking in scope** limited, narrow – 11 **unique** [ju:'ni:k] special, original – 14 **fine arts** literature, painting, sculpture, music, etc.

Sculpture, on the other hand, was taboo, so that even at the beginning of this century women sculptors were excluded from the academies of fine art. As for music, women were accepted in the reproductive sphere as singers and instrumentalists and also as teachers, but composition remained out of bounds to them.

There was no lack of attempts to explain the absence of woman's contribution to artistic production by referring to her "natural" creative deficit. Yet the many forgotten and disregarded works by women still hidden in the archives of music libraries prove this argument to be false. The difficulties of tracing these works are increased by the fact that many of the obviously unjustly neglected women composers published under male pseudonyms.

In the discussion about female creativity it is surprising that such a rigid division is made between apparently uncreative performance and creative composition. In reality this division is a blurred one. Singing and playing an instrument both demand creativity, for the personal interpretation of the performing artist is important to the impact of a piece. Women singers have moved their listeners to tears and earned passionate applause. Can such reactions really be achieved by mere imitation?

From "'Dolce semplice?' On the Changing Role of Women in Music" by Eva Rieger, translated by Harriet Anderson, in: *Feminist Aesthetics* edited by Gisla Ecker, London: The Women's Press (34 Great Sutton Street, London, EC1V ODX), 1985, p. 136.

6. The Image of Women in Advertising

Look in a mirror. If you are a woman, what do you see? A woman waxing a floor? Feeding children? Spraying her hair? Scribbling on a steno pad? Gazing at a man with mixed reverence and awe? The simple mirrors that hang over bureaus and on the backs of closet doors only tell us superficial physical things about ourselves. The real-life mirrors are the media, and for women the most invidious mirror of all is advertising.

19 **out of bounds** out of reach – 24 **to trace** *here:* to find out where s.th. is – 28 **rigid** not flexible – 31 **impact** ['ɪmpækt] effect
3 **to gaze** to stare – **reverence** great respect – **awe** [ɔ:] admiration – 4 **bureau** ['bjʊərəʊ] *here:* dresser – 5 **superficial** on the surface – 6 **invidious** [ɪn'vɪdɪəs] unfair

There once was some concern over the danger of subliminal advertising that would force people to make subconscious decisions about products or politics. Advertising today is not subliminal, but its subtle psychological effect is as devastating as any secret message flashed at high speeds to unsuspecting viewers. Advertising exploits and reinforces the myths of woman's place with messages of such infinite variety and number that one might as easily deny that the earth revolves around the sun as entirely reject their influence. Advertising is an insidious propaganda machine for a male supremacist society. It spews out images of women as sex mates, housekeepers, mothers and menial workers – images that perhaps reflect the true status of most women in society, but which also make it increasingly difficult for women to break out of the sexist stereotypes that imprison them.

Ironically, one hope remains: that the constant humiliating image of the role women are expected to play will draw their degradation in lines too bold and clear to ignore, and that women finally will arise in disgust and outrage to destroy the distortions reflected by that real-life mirror and to challenge the existence of sexism itself. [...]

Advertising did not create these images about women, but it is a powerful force for their reinforcement. It legitimizes the idealized, stereotyped roles of woman as temptress, wife, mother, and sex object, and portrays women as less intelligent and more dependent than men. It makes women believe that their chief role is to please men and that their fulfillment will be as wives, mothers, and homemakers. It makes women feel unfeminine if they are not pretty enough and guilty if they do not spend most of their time in desperate attempts to imitate gourmet cooks and eighteenth-century scullery maids. It makes women

8 **subliminal advertising** [ˌsʌbˈlɪmɪnl] advertising that affects the mind without the viewer being aware of it – 11 **devastating** [ˈdevəsteɪtɪŋ] destructive – 12 **unsuspecting** unprepared, trusting – **to exploit** to make use of s.th. in order to make money – **to reinforce** to strengthen – 14 **to deny** to say that s.th. is not true – 15 **to reject** to refuse to accept – 16 **insidious propaganda** propaganda whose influence develops unnoticeably but which has a very bad effect – **male supremacist society** [sʊˈpreməsɪst] society in which men have supremacy over women, i.e. more power – **to spew out** to throw out – 17 **menial workers** people who do hard and dirty work with their hands – 23 **disgust** strong feeling of disapproval – 24 **outrage** anger – **distortion** false, exaggerated image – 28 **temptress** woman who tempts men to fall in love with her, usu. without serious intentions – 33 **in desperate attempts** trying very hard, because it seems like your last hope – 34 **scullery maid** a low female servant

believe that their own lives, talents, and interests ought to be secondary to the needs of their husbands and families and that they are almost totally defined by these relationships.

It creates false, unreal images of women that reflect male fantasies rather than flesh and blood human beings. And the idealization of women is not much healthier than their derogation; goddesses are easily pulled off their pedestals and turned into temptresses and whores.

Advertising also reinforces men's concepts about women's place and women's role – and about their own roles. It makes masculine dominance legitimate – and conversely questions the manhood of men who do not want to go along with the stereotypes. Why is it masculine for men to wash cars, but a sign of "henpecking" for them to wash dishes? Why is it a man's job to be the breadwinner and a woman's to be the homemaker? Why do some men feel guilty when their wives work – as if it were a reflection on their own inadequacies? Advertising prolongs the myths of male supremacy, painting pictures of men who are superior to women and etching those images in the eyes of men who use these "eternal verities" as the excuse for forcing women's continued subjugation.

Male reactions to charges of sexism in advertising vary from defensive, "We didn't think that was degrading. ... It's a woman's role to care for the home," to the coldly, consciously contemptuous, "all women are masochists." "Insulting?" inquired William Judd, creative services manager for Parker Pen. "No, I would have to say that I don't recall that question coming up." He did get about ten letters complaining about the "Give her a gorgeous pen" ad. ("You might as well give her a gorgeous pen to keep her checkbook unbalanced with. A sleek and shining pen will make her feel prettier. Which is more important to any girl than solving mathematical mysteries.") He noted parenthetically that the ad was aimed at men. "It was a surprise to us that anyone felt that strongly about it. We still don't feel that this ad in any way was degrad-

41 **pedestal** ['---] platform for a statue – 42 **whore** [hɔ:] prostitute – 45 **conversely** [ˌkənˈvɜːslɪ] on the other hand – 50 **inadequacies** [ˌɪnˈædəkwəsɪz] shortcomings, faults – 54 **subjugation** oppression – 57 **contemptuous** without respect – 58 **to insult s.o.** to hurt s.o.'s feelings – 61 **gorgeous** very beautiful – 62 **to keep your checkbook balanced** to make sure you have enough money on your bank account to cover the checks you write

ing at all. You'd have to have a pretty thin skin to go away with that attitude."

From "The Image of Women in Advertising" by Lucy Komisar in *Woman in Sexist Society – Studies in Power and Powerlessness* edited by Vivian Gornick and Barbara K. Moran, New York: Basic Books, 1971, pp. 207, 211–212. Copyright © 1971 by Basic Books, Fnc. Reprinted by permission of Basic Books, a division of HarperCollins Publishers.